F1 History

The Billion Dollar Man Versus Mad Max

(The Years That Gave Rise to the Largest Motorsports Competition)

Alvena Hane

Published By **Tyson Maxwell**

Alvena Hane

All Rights Reserved

F1 History: The Billion Dollar Man Versus Mad Max (The Years That Gave Rise to the Largest Motorsports Competition)

ISBN 978-1-77485-895-0

No part of this guidebook shall be reproduced in any form without permission in writing from the publisher except in the case of brief quotations embodied in critical articles or reviews.

Legal & Disclaimer

The information contained in this ebook is not designed to replace or take the place of any form of medicine or professional medical advice. The information in this ebook has been provided for educational & entertainment purposes only.

The information contained in this book has been compiled from sources deemed reliable, and it is accurate to the best of the Author's knowledge; however, the Author cannot guarantee its accuracy and validity and cannot be held liable for any errors or omissions. Changes are periodically made to this book. You must consult your doctor or get professional medical advice before using any of the suggested remedies, techniques, or information in this book.

Upon using the information contained in this book, you agree to hold harmless the Author from and against any damages, costs, and expenses, including any legal fees potentially resulting from the application of any of the information provided by this guide. This disclaimer applies to any damages or injury caused by the use and application, whether directly or indirectly, of any advice or information presented, whether for breach of contract, tort, negligence, personal injury, criminal intent, or under any other cause of action.

You agree to accept all risks of using the information presented inside this book. You need to consult a professional medical practitioner in order to ensure you are both able and healthy enough to participate in this program.

TABLE OF CONTENTS

Introduction 1

Chapter 1: 1950: The Beginning Of It All .. 4

Chapter 2: 1954: The Return Of Fangio .. 12

Chapter 3: The Versatility Of Fangio And His Legend 15

Chapter 4: The Resurgence Of Ferrari 32

Chapter 5: Williams' Invasion Of Williams 42

Chapter 6: 2007 Return Of Ferrari 58

Chapter 7: Hamilton's Reign Mercedes And The Documents Of Hamilton 71

Introduction

Formula 1 is the obsession to be the fastest on the asphalt. It is the passion for that split second that separates success from failure. But what is it that we are so passionate about this sport that it can be summed up in a single word: speed?

Formula 1 is what you don't see before the green light: technology to polish that piece that allows you to start a few thousandths from the stopwatch; develop the most powerful engine to make the car fly on the track or control the wind to convert it into a few extra kilometers per hour through aerodynamics. Formula 1 is ingenuity and effort to get the fastest beast on the grid.

But Formula 1 is also what you see on the asphalt. Battles on the track on the border between life and death, overtaking outside the line at more than 300 km / h, devouring the pianos to the extreme assuming the risk of an accident or leaving the track ...

Formula 1 is also prestige, responsibility, brands risking their image and the honor of creating the most powerful vehicle on the face of the Earth.

But above all, Formula 1 is its history. I would not be covered with that halo of heroism without those who through control of time and speed became heroes on the asphalt.

The Fangio revolution, the Lotus years, Ferrari's eternal struggle through time, the rise of Williams, the rivalry between Ayrton Senna and Alain Prost, the legend of Kaiser Michael Schumacher, the best years of McLaren, Alonso and Renault , the dominance of Red Bull and Vettel, the super champion Hamilton and the hybrid era of Mercedes ...

Formula 1 would not be what it is without the glory of the past years poured into each of the great prizes, which bring memories of yesterday to our present. You don't enjoy this sport so much without knowing its route, its history, the greatness that one day was and will continue to be and that comes back to our minds every time the engines roar.

That is the objective of this book: a simple walk through its history so that every new Formula 1 fan can enjoy the origins and years that mythologized this sport, so that they feel the weight of history, thus adding one more dose of passion for the best motorsport championship today. It is also a walk for those who enjoyed their past and want to remember and bask in the blessed nostalgia for those races that will never return.

Because Formula 1 continually changes, but the passion always remains. I hope you enjoy this journey through time and that these keys make you know, remember and enjoy even more the passion of this sport.

Let the engines start!

Chapter 1: 1950: The Beginning Of It All

On May 13, 1950, in Great Britain, at the Silverstone circuit, the single-seaters began to roll, beginning a championship that would grow in importance until creating the passion that Formula 1 is today for all its fans.

Previously, the European Drivers' Championship had already been established in 1931, unifying several of the most important grands prix that previously acted as independent events. However, after six editions, the irruption of World War II ended up making the championship disappear.

After the war, the AIACR (Association Internationale des Automobile Clubs Reconnus), was reorganized giving rise to the FIA (International Automobile Federation), establishing the rules of a new Formula 1: 4.5-liter atmospheric or supercharged 1 ,5 liters. For 1950, the first Drivers' World Championship was organized, bringing together six of the most important grands prix.

In this first edition the calendar would consist of the great prizes of Great Britain (Silverstone), Monaco (Monte Carlo), Switzerland (Bremgarten), Belgium (Spa), France (Reims-Gueux) and Italy (Monza). Due to its impact, the Indianapolis 500 would also be included as a scoring event. Only the first five drivers scored (counting only their best four races) plus an additional point for the fastest lap, and if two drivers had to share the same vehicle, the points were shared.

The Mercedes-Benz or Auto Union, German vehicles that had dominated before the war, were missed at the opening of the championship.

However, everything was ready and the first edition of the Formula 1 Drivers' World Championship began.

Giuseppe Farina, the first champion

Italian Giuseppe Farina would be the first driver to cross the finish line in a world championship race by taking first place at Silverstone. This would make him the first driver to achieve a victory in this sport.

This victory, together with that of Switzerland and Italy, would also lead him at 44 to win the championship title, extending his feat to become the first champion of a Formula 1 world competition.

He would do it aboard the Alfa Romeo 158, a voiturette that was invincible as this team achieved the six championship victories on European soil.

The main rival of Nino Farina for the championship was the Argentine Juan Manuel Fangio, who only managed to lead by three points. The third classified was the Italian Luigi Fagioli, being the three Alfa Romeo drivers, thus demonstrating the power of this team in this first edition of the championship.

Monaco, 1950, the debut of a historical: Ferrari

It wasn't until the second race of the World Drivers' Championship that Scuderia Ferrari made an appearance in the competition. Although he could not attend the first appointment at Silverstone, the prestigious Italian team debuted on May 21 in Monaco. Since then, she would become the only one today to participate in all editions of the championship.

The best positioned driver for Ferrari in this first season was Alberto Ascari, finishing sixth in the final standings with 11 points. Ascari achieved second place in Monaco and Monza (in the latter with Dorino Serafini). Luigi Villoresi, Raymond Sommer, Dorino Serafini and Peter Whitehead were also on its squad.

Ferrari participated in this edition with the 125, 275 and 375 models.

1951: Fangio's revenge

The second season of the World Championship began as the first ended, with Alfa Romeo dominating its rivals. However, throughout the championship, Ferrari was improving its development while Alfa remained stagnant, finding a dangerous rival in the Scuderia. In fact, Ferrari had already shown its ability to compete in the non-scoring grand prix before the start of the championship.

At the British Grand Prix, Alfa Romeo showed its weakness when it comes to fuel efficiency, having to make two pit stops, which allowed the Ferrari of Argentine José Froilán González to win.
Alfa Romeo was defeated for the first time on European soil and Ferrari achieved its first victory in the championship.

After the victory of José Froilán González, the two consecutive Ascari in Germany and

Italy would come, leaving Fangio only two points ahead for the last race of the season: Spain. Ascari got the pole for the last grand prix, however a wrong choice of tires made Fangio win the race and therefore the championship at 40 years old, becoming the second champion of the competition and obtaining his little personal revenge against his partner Farina, who would be fourth.

Ferrari and Ascari fill Alfa Romeo void
The main surprise in the third edition of the championship was the absence of Alfa Romeo, a team that had achieved victory in the first two editions. The Italian government refused to finance a new car and this led to the withdrawal of the team.

This endangered the competitiveness of the championship, as Ferrari was left without competition and with relative superiority. To avoid this, the FIA adopted the rules of Formula 2, forcing Ferrari to regulate its superior 4.5-liter engine. By adopting cheaper regulation, more teams were also expected to join.

Following the withdrawal of Alfa Romeo, Farina accepted Ferrari's offer, but had to do so under the shadow of Ascari. For his part, an accident by Fangio in a non-scoring event at Monza prevented him from participating in the championship.

Thus the things and in spite of the attempts of the FIA to obtain the equality, Ferrari dominated and through Ascari it gained six of the seven tests in European territory. He only did not get the victory in Switzerland and because he did not participate as he was preparing the 500 Miles. Absolute dominance of Ascari, who was proclaimed champion at 34, and first Ferrari title.

The following year, also under Formula 2 regulations, Ferrari would once again be the undisputed leader. Ascari won the first three races of the championship (not counting the 500 Miles) bringing the number of consecutive victories to 9, and would win two more to claim his second world title.

His winning streak would only be interrupted by Mike Hawthorn, also for Ferrari. The Englishman had earned a place in the team after his good work in the previous season.

Farina would manage to win the German Grand Prix to be third in the championship, and Fangio would emerge victorious from Italy, aboard the Maserati, to get the runner-up and avoid the full of triumphs for Ferrari.

This season would be characterized as the first to include a race on South American soil, the Argentine Grand Prix in Buenos Aires. However, she would be remembered for the tragedy in which 9 people died after an accident.

F1-web.com.ar

Chapter 2: 1954: The Return Of Fangio

If anyone could end the hegemony of Ferrari, that was Juan Manuel Fangio. Thus, the Argentine achieved victory in the opening race of the 1954 season on his own land. In Belgium he would win the victory again with Maserati, hitting the table.

Then, Fangio went on to drive for Mercedes Benz, which made its debut in France and did so in a spectacular way, with a great advantage over its rivals and getting a double thanks to Fangio and Karl Kling. However, at Silverstone the Mercedes accused the aerodynamics and gave Ferrari a break, which returned the double on British soil.

Mercedes learned from mistakes and redesigned the chassis in a show of German efficiency, leading to Fangio winning the next three races (Germany, Switzerland and Italy) and leading the Argentine to his second world title.

Hawthorn closed the season with an insufficient victory at Monza for Ferrari, which had found a formidable rival in Mercedes, despite the fact that its drivers José Froilán González had secured the runner-up and Hawthorn third place.

1955: The Le Mans disaster

In 1955 a rule change extended to five the maximum races of the championship in which a pilot could score, thus accounting for his five best performances of the eleven possible after the return from Monaco and Holland.

However, a tragedy changed the course of the competition: the Le Mans disaster. On June 11 at the Circuit de la Sarthe, during the legendary 24 Hours of Le Mans race, an accident killed the driver Pierre Levegh and 83 spectators, being considered the worst tragedy in motorsports.

Although the race was not suspended (and Mike Hawthorn would eventually win it), the races in France, Germany, Spain and Switzerland were suspended, altering the calendar of the Formula 1 World Championship.

These changes would not alter the trend of the competition, in which Fangio was once again the most prominent along with Mercedes, winning 5 of the 7 races held and comfortably obtaining his third world title (second in a row), thus expanding his legend.

Chapter 3: The Versatility Of Fangio And His Legend

After the withdrawal of Mercedes after the disaster at Le Mans, Ferrari did not miss the option of returning to dominate the orbit of Formula 1: sign Fangio. The Argentine complied from the beginning by winning the first race, although he had to do it with his teammate Luigi Musso's car after a breakdown in his own.

However, things for Fangio weren't easy at all. Stirling Moss, who would eventually be remembered as the best performing driver ever to win a championship title, showed remarkable consistency by winning two races with Maserati. Both BRM and Vanwall also performed well in the race.

However, the biggest threat to Fangio was his teammate Peter Collins, who was only 8 points ahead of the last race of the championship: Monza. If Fangio did not score and Collins managed to win, in addition to the fastest lap, the title would go to the British.

Already in the race, Fangio had a breakdown in his vehicle, so he suggested using that of his partner Luigi Musso as the only alternative to continue. The Italian refused, but then it was Collins himself, in a remarkable act of sportsmanship and respect within the team, who gave his car to Fangio, who would finish second in the race adding his fourth world title (third in a row), this time with Ferrari, thus demonstrating its versatility.

In 1957, Fangio changed teams again, this time joining Maserati. This turned out to be a wise decision, as Ferrari diminished its performance and was unable to achieve victory in any of the grand prixes.

The sporting decline joined the personal tragedy after the death of two of its drivers out of competition: the Italian Eugenio Castelloti and Alfonso de Portago, the first

Spanish driver who had managed to drive for Ferrari.

This season, Fangio found his main competitor in Stirling Moss, who after signing for Vanwall, managed to win three races to return to runner-up behind Fangio, who won four victories. The Argentine thus achieved his fifth world title (once again with a different car), and fourth in a row.

At the end of the season, Fangio announced his retirement with five world titles, having forged a legend in Formula 1. In the same way, Maserati also abandoned due to its financial situation.

1958: The World Constructors' Championship and the most tragic season

In 1958, the FIA created the World Constructors' Championship for the first time. The brands thus acquired another incentive to compete by adding professional prestige beyond trying to lead one of their pilots to the title.

However, despite this initiative, the 1958 season would be remembered for being the most tragic in Formula 1 when four drivers died in four different races.

Luigi Musso, Ferrari driver, would lose his life at the French Grand Prix (Reims). His partner Peter Collins would do it in Germany (Nürburgring). Stuart Lewins-Evans, a Vanwall driver, would suffer an accident in Morocco and American Pat O'Connor would die in Indianapolis.

In the sports part, Mike Hawthorn would take advantage of the first season of the post Fangio era to win the title driving the Ferrari 143 2.4 V6. After getting the title, he would retire from the championship although, paradoxically, he would end up dying months later in a traffic accident.

Despite the victory of the Ferrari driver, the first constructors' title would go to Vanwall, thanks to the performances of Stirling Moss (runner-up once again), Tony Brooks and the late Stuart Lewis-Evans, who knew how to take advantage of the Vanwall's performance 254 2.5 L4 to get 6 victories throughout the championship.

The abandonment of the front engines

In 1959, most of the vehicles abandoned the front engine, changing it for one in the central position (except for Ferrari, which would take time to move its engine until 1961). In this new change, Cooper surprised with his 2.5-liter rear Coventry Climax engine, which, driven by Jack Brabham, Stirling Moss and Bruce McLaren, would end up taking the constructors' title by achieving victory in five races.

Of their drivers, both Brabham and Moss had options in the last race in the United States to be named champions, along with Tony Brooks of Ferrari. Moss had to retire due to technical problems, once again on the verge of success.

Brabham, for his part, ran out of gas, being forced to push his car... to cross the finish line and become world champion.

The following year, 1960, was the last of the 2.5-liter engines. The trend would be continuous from the previous year, with no changes beyond eliminating the point per fast lap and expanding the scoring positions to six.

Cooper would dominate even more comfortably than the previous season, winning his second consecutive constructors' title, and with victory again for Jack Brabham, who would add his second championship.

This season the upgrade of rear-engined teams was confirmed, with Lotus, BRM and Porsche prevailing over front-engined cars.

It was also the last year that the Indianapolis 500 was eligible for the Formula 1 championship.

1.5 liter engines

1961 was the first year of the 1.5-liter engines, a change to which Ferrari, together with the adoption of the rear engine, adapted more quickly, judging by the absolute dominance in the competition.

The Italian team won five of the eight races, and only Lotus was able to beat them. Ferrari thus managed to return to the top by winning the constructors' title and among its drivers, Phil Hill would be the first American to achieve a world title.
In the French Grand Prix, the pilot Giancarlo Baghetti would achieve the feat of winning a race with a private vehicle, made by Ferrari. This is somewhat more impressive considering that it was his debut in the competition.

Nor would he be spared this season of tragedy when, at Monza, Wolfgang von Trips collided with Jim Clark, blowing the German's car through the air, killing him and 14 fans.

The British rise

Ferrari's victory in 1960 would be a fleeting success, as in 1961 the team was overwhelmed by the push of the British teams. Despite the good start to the season, the Italian team suffered a strike in the middle of the championship that forced them not to participate in the last two Grand Prix.

Ferrari's void was quickly filled by BRM (British Racing Motors), who won both the constructors 'and drivers' titles, which would go to Graham Hill. The British driver would get four victories that would lead him to win the championship.

BRM's biggest rival was Lotus, which at the hands of Jim Clark, surprised by its monocoque design, being the first Formula 1 manufactured in a single piece.

For its part, the Porsche team would achieve its first (and only) victory in a grand prix at the hands of the American Dan Gurney in France (Rouen).

Also noteworthy is the role of Jack Brabham, who managed to score points this time with his own team.

As for Stirling Moss, he had signed for Ferrari but an accident prior to the championship prevented him from contesting the season, and in fact he would no longer compete in a Formula 1 Grand Prix. The "champion without a crown", one of the drivers with the best results without ever winning the world title.

In 1963 it would be a British team that would get the constructors' title. This time it would be Lotus, which had already surprised by its monocoque design, and now it was also with its performance. The Lotus-Climax team would also lead the British driver Jim Clark to win the championship, setting the record of winning seven races in the same season.

The 1964 season featured a very close match between Jim Clark, Graham Hill and John Surtees. The three pilots, British, thus showed the rise of the United Kingdom in the competition. In the last race, Hill collided with Lorenzo Bandini's Ferrari while Clark suffered an oil leak that forced him to stop. Thus, Surtees ended up becoming the world champion.

John Surtees was proclaimed champion aboard a Ferrari, which also achieved the constructors' title, rising again to the top. Surtees got the title thanks to the fact that, with team orders, his teammate Bandini let him pass on the last lap.

In 1965 the Lotus-Clark duo returned to achieve success. The Lotus team won its second constructors 'title, while Jim Clark also won his second (and last) drivers' title.

Clark got the victory in six of the first seven races, he only needed to win in Monaco, which he did not appear because he was preparing the Indianapolis 500, which by the way he also managed to win.

1965 would also be remembered as the year in which Honda would get its first victory (after having debuted the previous year), and it would do so in Mexico with Richie Ginther.

1966: 3-liter engines

In 1966 the engine capacity was doubled to 3 liters. In addition, a new rule was established that it was necessary to complete at least 90% of the race to score points, and the maximum mileage of these was reduced from 500 to 400 kilometers.

The changes allowed Australian Jack Brabham to win the drivers 'world title again for the second time, and his team,

Brabham-Repco, to win the constructors' title.

Brabham won four consecutive races leading to the title. John Surtees, who was runner-up, won the second race of the season with Ferrari, and also the last, but with Cooper-Maserati.
The following year, in 1967 Brabham-Repco would once again win the constructors' title, obtaining its second and last title.

However, the drivers' title went to New Zealander Denny Hulme, Jack Brabham's teammate, although he would end up being runner-up. The funny thing about Hulme is that he would be the first driver to be proclaimed champion without having achieved any pole. Jim Clark, despite achieving four victories with Lotus, could only finish third.

This season, at the Dutch Grand Prix, Lotus used one of the most victorious engines in history, the Ford Cosworth DFV.

For his part, Mexican Pedro Rodríguez de la Vega would get Cooper's last victory in the South African Grand Prix.

Already in the following season, in 1968, Lotus asserted its commitment to the Ford Cosworth engine and returned to the top with its third manufacturer's title. He would do so by leading Britain's Graham Hill to win the drivers' championship after winning three races, the same as his top competitor Jackie Stewart.

The glory of Jackie Stewart and the aerodynamic changes

In 1969, the Matra brand decided to focus exclusively on the Matra International team, boosting the team in competitiveness to the point of claiming the constructors 'title, leading Jackie Stewart to win his first drivers' championship.

Matra's achievement is remarkable since he had started to compete the previous season, and once the competition had already started. It marks the first victory for a French team and a vehicle with a chassis made in France. For more glory, Stewart nearly doubled second-placed Jacky Ickx's Brabham in points.

This season the use of ailerons was prohibited due to their danger, although they would end up being allowed again, but with weight and size restrictions and as long as they were attached to the chassis and not to the suspensions.

There is also a special attraction for 4x4 traction, although only one car with traction would score points and in fact most drivers hated driving this type of vehicle. Ford further discovered that its engine was efficient when power was transmitted to the rear wheels.

Other technical changes that became important were the use of wide wheels and the use of the ground effect in order to achieve more grip.
The posthumous title of Jochen Rindt

In 1970, Lotus once again demonstrated its constant competitiveness and once again won the constructors' title by winning 6 of the 13 races. He did it thanks to the Austrian pilot Jochen Rindt, who achieved victory in five grands prix that would earn him the drivers' title. He would achieve it, sadly, posthumously when he died in the Italian Grand Prix practice before finishing the championship that he would end up winning, this being the only case with these characteristics throughout the history of the competition.

Jackie Stewart adds and goes

In 1971, Jackie Stewart would be proclaimed champion again, this time aboard a Tyrrell team car, the first and only time that he would manage to lift the constructors' title. Stewart also beat with relative ease, leading by 29 points to his immediate pursuer, the Swede Ronnie Peterson who was driving for March.

Fitipaldi's meddling and one more from Lotus

In 1972, Stewart would find a great rival who would intrude on his glory: the Brazilian Emerson Fittipaldi. With five victories compared to the four of the British driver, Fittipaldi would be proclaimed champion, also giving the fifth constructors' title to Lotus, demonstrating once again its ability to always be on top.

In 1973 the battle between Stewart and Fittipaldi would continue. This time it would be the British who, with six victories compared to the three of the Brazilian, would end up proclaiming himself champion, getting his third title. He would do it one more time aboard a Tyrrell.

However, he could not prevent the constructors' championship from being once again for Lotus, as Fittipaldi would be second in the classification and his partner, the Swede Peterson, third, obtaining the sixth title of Lotus for legend of the team.

In 1974, Stewart retired after the death of his partner François Cevert, a fact that affected him emotionally. The British left the competition with three titles achieved. This deprived us of a new fight against Emerson Fittipaldi, who ended up proclaiming himself champion once again, obtaining his second and last world title.

He would get it after his signing for McLaren, who would get his first constructors' title under the name McLaren-Ford. It was not easy to get the final victory, as he achieved it with only three points of advantage over the Swiss Clay Regazzoni, who was driving for a Ferrari team that was missing the victories.

Chapter 4: The Resurgence Of Ferrari

In 1975, Ferrari would manage to rise again to the top. It would not be with the Swiss Regazzoni, who had been runner-up the previous season, but with a historical name in Formula 1: Niki Lauda.

The Austrian led Fittipaldi by almost 20 points to win the drivers 'title and give the Italian team its long-awaited third constructors' title.

The following year, in 1976, Lauda missed the championship by a single point, and it went to the British James Hunt, who won his only world title driving for McLaren-Ford. This year was the fateful season in which Lauda had the brutal accident that disfigured his face and in which many doctors even announced his death. Despite missing several races because of it and in pain because of the injuries with his helmet bloody every time he had to use it, he came back to try to come back, although he was finally only one point behind his great rival Hunt.

Ferrari would at least manage to keep the constructors' title, fourth for the Italian team.

He would not miss his second title in 1977, with a notable advantage over South African driver Jody Scheckter. Ferrari would also be proclaimed champion as a team: fifth title for the Italian team.

The latest from Lotus and the ground effect

If the history of Formula 1 has shown us anything so far, it is that Lotus had always been there. And if anyone could end the dominance of Lauda and Ferrari, it was the British team. Thus, at the hands of the American Mario Andretti, the team achieved its seventh title, which unfortunately would be the last for the prestigious brand that would have contributed so much to the first years of the competition.

The success of Lotus was due in large part to the implementation of the "ground effect" in its car for the first time. It is due to an aerodynamic effect of the air that circulates around the car that generates a pressure difference over and under the vehicle in a way that "crushes" it, fixing it to the ground and, above all, allowing higher speeds when cornering.

The new cornering speed coupled with the few means to control it made this effect turn into a deadly effect, so the FIA in 1981 banned the aerodynamic skirts and in 1983 forced the flat bottom that finally ended the practice of the effect ground.

This season, Niki Lauda had chosen to race with Brabham this season, which earned him a total of nine retirements. Despite the fact that the seven grands prix that he did finish did so on the podium, he could not be more than fourth in the final classification.

In 1979, Lotus would deflate. His best position in the final classification would be the seventh position of the Argentine Reutemann, with the champion Andretti descending to twelfth position.

Ferrari would take advantage of it to win its sixth constructors' title, leading South African Jody Scheckter to the top, who would beat his teammate Gilles Villeneuve by four points in an absolute dominance of the Italian team.

1980: Williams' first

In the 1980 season another of the historic teams entered the scene: Williams. Australian Alan Jones won his first (and only) drivers 'title, in the same way that the Williams-Ford team made its debut in the constructors' title.
 The most notable was the crash at Ferrari in which Gilles Villeneuve finish 14th in the final standings for their attempt to defend the title. Scheckter 19th.
When 1981 came around, Williams was back in 1981 to take home the constructor's title, in the end, he failed to earn the

driver's title, making the driver Reutemann in second place (just one point from that record) in second place, and Alan Jones third (two points further behind that championship).

The highly-contested year was won by Brazilian Nelson Piquet driving for Brabham winning the award. It was this driver's first championship.

Twitter.com

The next year, 1982, the opposite scenario would happen. Williams could guide the driver he has chosen to the title of world champion however he could not be able to win the constructors' title. The winner would be Finn Keke Rosberg who with one victory could be declared the world champion.

The constructors' championship will be yet again a win for Ferrari and Ferrari, including Frenchman Didier Pironi making a name for himself among the other drivers as well as Mario Andretti and Gilles Villeneuve getting eliminated from the final standings.

Ferrari would again be able to validate its title, this time in 1983 due to the two French racers: Rene Arnoux and Patrick

Tambay however, the drivers title would be handed in the name of Nelson Piquet, who would win his second title through Brabham.

In this year's season the performance that played by Alain Prost stood out, which demonstrates the rising popularity of French drivers. They are just two points ahead of the leader with Renault.

Resurrection of Niki Lauda, and the growth of Prost

The revolving door of Ferrari, Williams and Piquet was eventually quelled through the partnership between McLaren along with Porsche. The McLaren-TAG Porsche Turbo Team took home the constructors' trophy and also brought Austrian Niki Lauda to the top of his game. Lauda took home the last championship he won which was his third championship of his career.

This year's season will have been remembered as the fight against Niki Lauda and Alain Prost. The Frenchman only a half point away from winning the title after finishing second.

After two runners-up Alain Prost did not want to see third place and took home the crown in 1985. He won the title by a large margin, while his teammate and rival Niki Lauda fell to 10th place. But, McLaren once again revalidated the manufacturer's title.

On the other hand, Brazilian Ayrton Senna began to appear in the distance in the fourth position on the Lotus. Lotus.
It was in 1986 that Prost took home his 2nd world championship, this time, he faced more challenges. Prost was only able to surpass Nigel Mansell and his Williams by two points. They was forced to withdraw at the end of the season, even though Prost would win the championship. Frenchman ended up winning the championship. In the back, Nelson Piquet was three points off the championship with Williams-Honda which could help the team to claim the title of constructors. Senna along with Lotus was fourth in the race.
Aporlacopa.blogspot.com
As of 1987 Prost could be fourth place in rankings, giving an advantage to his competitors and of whom Nelson Piquet

was the one who took the greatest advantage the Williams to win his third and final world title. Nigel Mansell would return to second place and Senna would climb to third place.
Diariomotor.com

Ayrton Senna Alain Prost and McLaren
In the latest fight in the recent fight between Williams as well as McLaren and their varying the past few years of success, McLaren had not said his last words and took an exciting Ayrton Senna Lotus who won his first title at the world championship in 1988 before returning in first place with McLaren at the time of the constructors championship.

McLaren's dominance was staggering winning fifteen of 16 race. This is something that's not shocking, given that he was in the team two outstanding drivers, such as Ayrton Senna (who was victorious in 8 races) and Alan Prost (who was victorious in seven races) . Between them , they scored more points than all the other six teams.

The Senna-Prost duo remained as successful in 1989 this was a logical repeat of the previous season but with a difference that this time, it was the French who won the title , while it was the Brazilian who finished second. The third class, Ricardo Patrese, was 20 points lower than the second classification, with Williams. Williams.

In this race, engines that were supercharged were banned , and it was decided that the driver's feet had to be in front of the wheels to shield leg muscles in the case in the event of an incident. The race distance was limited to 305 km in order to ensure a maximum of time to two hours.

Due to the high number of entries Due to the large number of entries, a qualifying race was set up with only 30 drivers participating at the event. The changes, as was seen didn't affect the dominance of McLaren.

In the year 1990, Alain Prost signed for Ferrari and his position was filled by Austrian Gerhard Berger. This increased competition in the constructor class and added Ferrari to the fight however in the individual situation, the rivalry was still fought among Prost and Senna who again beat their competitors by 30 points.

In this particular edition the title was returned to Brazil's control and Ayrton Senna was able to surpass that of his teammate Alain Prost. The title for the constructors regardless of the effort made by Ferrari as well as Nigel Mansell, continued in the hands of the mighty McLaren-Honda team.

The 1991 winners were repeated. Ayrton Senna took home his third and final driver championship. McLaren-Honda retained its dominance with the constructors championship.

Nigel Mansell, with Williams was second, still a considerable distance ahead of the Brazilian champion. Alain Prost was fourth with his Ferrari.

Chapter 5: Williams' Invasion Of Williams

Pinterest.com

Following Mclaren's relentless success, Williams became the alternative and in 1992, he was able to take the lead by winning the constructors' championship and ahead of Nigel Mansell, finally and after a string of runners-up, to take home the coveted title of world champion.

Topgear.es

Mansell's advantage was significant in winning 9 grand prix and more than doubling in points the second class Riccardo Patrese, his co-teammate. However although sharing a vehicle was not able to get as close to his performances.

Michael Schumacher's third-place finish is a highlight of the season. He is 23 and working for Benetton. It was a prelude to the next season. Senna was fourth in McLaren in a year in which Alain Prost had decided to take a break from.

Alain Prost would return in 1993, and it appears that he had breaks that were not as useful, as it allowed him to get back to the top, and, after signing with Williams-Renault the team would win his fourth and final title before his final retirement.

Pinterest.com.mx

His co-driver on Williams will be Damon Hill, who would be third in the final class and allow Williams to be able to reinstate the title of constructor. In addition, Ayrton Senna would make it into the race, using an McLaren that didn't quit despite losing the battle for supremacy. Michael Schumacher continued to add kilometers along with Benetton and finished fourth.

The Kaiser's origins and Senna's goodbye

Michael Schumacher had already been enjoying very impressive results for an organization that was not thought to be to be among the champions. However, what transpired in 1994, when he declared his own champion after just 25 years at Benetton is a good example of the unending potential of Michael Schumacher. German pilot.

Michael Schumacher came just one point ahead from Damon Hill in the final race of the season in Australia. Both drivers resigned in the Australian Grand Prix meant victory in the championship for the German driver.

As a legend was beginning to be created, another racer died during the San Marino Grand Prix in Imola. Ayrton Senna's car left straight on the Tamburello turn during lap 7 and crashed into the wall of concrete at 218 km/h. Even after his admission into the medical center in Bologna there was nothing that could be taken in order to save his life. Senna lost a champion who won three world championships and an Formula 1 legend.

Ran.de

In the next season, Michael Schumacher repeated the world championship, proving that his feat was not a result of luck. Actually the second time, he was capable of leading the Benetton team to win the constructors' championship thanks to the assistance to Johnny Herbert, who finished fourth in the race, scoring less than half the points as Schumacher. German. Damon Hill was runner-up again however this time he was just 33 points back of Schumacher. David Coulthard, his teammate at Williams was able to secure third place, but could not get enough points to catch Benetton following Schumacher's heroics.

Williams against. Schumacher-Ferrari
In 1996, Ferrari had the chance to finalize the deal with the gifted Michael Schumacher, seeking with this remarkable driver to bring his style on the track in Formula 1 after many years in the shade of teams like Williams as well as McLaren.
It's not clear if it was a smart choice, as the following retirements of six (although getting three wins), Michael could not be more than third in the final class.
Damon Hill would not waste the chance to end up behind the German and win his first driver's championship (becoming his first winner son the champion) with a score of twelve points higher than his teammate Jacques Villeneuve, on the record of Williams was always setting the pace, but was stopped by Michael Schumacher who had burst into the race, completely unexpectedly, winning the constructors' championship.
Redbull.com

Schumacher's teammate from Ferrari, Briton Eddie Irvine was ranked 10th in the standings with 11 retirements indicating that Michael did not have an engine that was reliable enough to secure the championship. Actually, the drivers from his previous Benetton team finished third (Alesi) in addition to sixth (Bergher) The issue is whether Schumacher would have been able to beat Williams once more with his former team.

As of 1997 Williams maintained its position as the most popular team, was again crowned the builder ' and drivers title with this time the Canadian Jacques Villeneuve before Hill's marches to Arrows.

Villeneuve had to contend with Michael Schumacher who this time had a better Ferrari and actually was first in the final race in the world championship at Jerez. Michael tried to trigger an accident on his own to stop the Canadian from taking over his position however he finished 3rd in the event, declaring himself the champion, and the German having to pull out. Because of his actions Michael was disqualified by the FIA removed Michael's place as third place.

McLaren comes back to his role

In the wake of Williams taking over the stage, and Schumacher becoming the idea of a Ferrari capable of competing for another title In 1998, one of the greatest teams comes back to the scene: McLaren, with Mercedes engines.

With 100 points Finn Mika Hakkinen scored 100 points. Finn Mika Hakkinen took home the title of driver and, with Coulthard's points (third in the championship) they also awarded McLaren another constructors title.

Ferrari became McLaren's most formidable rival McLaren's biggest rival, Michael Schumacher finishing second, fourteen points ahead of the winner along with Eddie Irvine fourth. The Williamses were, on the other hand were able to get to the third place but were still well behind the top two teams. Villeneuve was fifth, and Frentzen seventh.

In 1999, the war against McLaren and Ferrari was rekindled, and they ended up with them having a shared title. Hakkinen was able to win his second consecutive win, however, this time it was the Italian team that would be the winner of the constructors' title.

Michael Schumacher, who had not yet exploded with Ferrari and was forced to miss six grand prix following the worst crash that he has ever had during the race in Great Britain, so he is substituted with Mika Salo. However, the German is able to keep fifth in the standings, and the teammate Eddie Irvine takes the runner-up with only two points behind Hakkinen. We'll never be able to know what Michael would have achieved in the event he hadn't missed six races.

Williams continues to fall apart and falls to fifth place among the constructors' rankings and has Italian Zanardi as well as Ralf Schumacher (Michael's brother) as the drivers. They are a bit surprised by the top positions in the top two positions of Jordan and Stewart who are fourth and third in the classification.

The Schumacher dictatorship
It was only in 2000, following four seasons of failure with Ferrari and Ferrari, the year

that Michael Schumacher would finally win the title of world champion by partnering with an Italian team. This was inevitable according to his talents.

In the grandstand, the fight among Ferrari and McLaren continued, which was far ahead of the other teams. Schumacher was battling McLaren's two McLaren and McLaren, both Hakkinen and Coulthard who finished third and second all the way through the championship, but the four consecutive wins in the last grand prix awarded Schumacher the prized the title of red.

Teammate and teammate Brazilian Rubens Barrichello scored enough points to allow Ferrari to win the title of constructor.

Williams was signed by the British team of Jenson Button, has climbed to third in the season, and is recovering somewhat but still far from Ferrari as well as McLaren.

The pattern in 2001 was not just a continuation of the same direction However, the dominance of Ferrari was more evident. Schumacher could take home nine victories (none of his rival Barrichello) as opposed to just two wins for Coulthard.

This means that Michael almost doubled the second place Briton in points. Ferrari also added 179 points to Mclaren's which opened up a gap between the two. In the meantime, Williams closed the gap to McLaren third in the standings.

Diariomotor.com

The 2002 dominance of Ferrari and Schumacher will be harder if it is it was possible. Schumacher would add points for his teammate Barrichello 2nd classified as well as his Italian team would add a double score of the second classed team and eventually change into Williams and, was, in addition to Ralf Schumacher and Ralf Schumacher, also had one of the Colombian Juan Pablo Montoya.

McLaren, on the other hand, McLaren accused the withdrawal of Hakkinen and, despite having a skilled Kimi Raikkonen along with Coulthard The team dropped to third place, dropping several points.

In 2003, scoring positions were increased to eight positions, and there was no limits on the scoring of races. This modification did not impact Michael Schumacher who once again took home the title of world champion with Ferrari, finishing fourth in succession with Ferrari and sixth in personal. While the Italian team was able to regain the constructors' title it was not able to display the same authority as the previous years, and showed the first indications of weak spots.

This was proved by the controversy over the drivers title, in which Kimi Raikkonen and McLaren could still be in contention during the race that would decide her fate in Japan and was only two points behind that of the German Six-time winner.

Matraxlubricantes.com

The gap between constructors decreased. Ferrari had only 14 points better than Williams and second in class and only two points higher than third-placed McLaren. This was the beginning of a championship that was not led by Ferrari however, it was only three points. In the back, all teams were quite ahead however Renault ended the season with 88 points, a excellent season.

In 2004 Formula 1 expanded in Asia through the addition of Formula 1's Bahrain Grand Prix and the Chinese Grand Prix, thus growing its market share as a representative of the grand racing business. This was which was accentuated by the presence of Bernie Ecclestone, who since the the 1970s, when the British magnate was able to purchase the rights to broadcast and Chinese Grand Prix, had had control of the finances of the competition and was in control of his ability to make money, up until 2017 when it was taken over by Liberty Media company.

While focusing on the sporting plane 2004 is the year which Schumacher ended a fantastic season with Ferrari and won the fifth consecutive win for the team and the seventh place in the German personal record which is a record that has remained unbeaten.

Although the previous season appeared to have been even across teams and at the very least within the top three teams, Ferrari re-dominated as it was doing a few several years ago with a win over second-ranked Ferrari by an average of 143 points.

In the team, things are not likely to change too significantly. Schumacher was the most prominent driver with a record of 13 wins. In Monaco Schumacher was forced to withdraw and he finished with a podium finish on the podium in Belgium in addition to Italy. The 12th position on the podium in China and seventh place in Brazil ended a remarkable year.

On the other hand, Rubens Barrichello, had to settle again for being his squire under with the German and ended up second, just 32 points back of the Kaiser.

Thebestf1.es

Although Ferrari's dominance was not as strong like the previous two years shock this year was for the other teams. Williams dropped to fourth position and McLaren fell to fifth. What teams did you not expect to slip over the two legends who took their spots?

The third class was Renault (which was already in the process of ceasing to be Benetton from 2001) it was a little bit of a shock because the previous year it had been performing fairly well. This was due to the young Alonso who, at 23 years old, he was able to achieve fourth position in the standings. He also scored four podiums and placing in the top 7 positions, except for the five grand prix he had to leave.

The year before, he already won his first race and had three podiums with Renault in Hungary following his signing with an French team (the prior year, he made his debut with Minardi in Formula 1 with Minardi) which showed his ability. In 2003, he finished at the sixth position in the standings and a bright future was awaiting for the young driver.

Teammate Jarno Trulli was sixth in the race with 46 points to round out the excellent season for Mild Seven Renault.

Es.wikipedia.org

Another team that wowed fans in 2004 was the BAR-Honda squad, comprising Jenson Button (third spot in the championship in the world) as well as The Japanese Takuma Sato (eighth).

Alonso and the ending of the Ferrari-Schumacher era

Es.wikipedia.org

Five years after the total dominance over Ferrari due the efforts of Michael Schumacher, it was difficult to imagine that Schumacher's reign could end quickly, or even in the near term. In this case the year 2005 Fernando Alonso and Renault emerged to end the dynasty that was that Italian team. The paradoxes of the fate of Schumacher had his record of 5 consecutive World Cups broken by the mark that earned Schumacher the chance to win his debut World Cup.

There were a number of regulations that could have impacted the final days of Ferrari's rule. The most important rule was the rule was that it wasn't permitted to change tires at pit stops (except for punctures or rain-like appearance). The engines, in turn, were required to be used in two consecutive grand prixs instead of one race. A significant aerodynamic change was also added to the wings to make use of the slipstream, making taking overtaking more easy.

If the change was due to the modifications or it was due to the changes or not, Michael Schumacher finished third in the final standings and was beaten in addition to the champion Alonso and Kimi Raikkonen, racing for McLaren. Ferrari's performance deteriorated in Barrichello's eighth place and, therefore, Schumacher is likely to have squeezed the best from the car, taking home a single win at America. United States.

In the other half of the teams McLaren gained positions and, in between the Raikkonens and Juan Pablo Montoya (who had to be substituted with Pedro de la Rosa and Wurz in two races) they were battling for the title along with Renault until the final race.

Ferrari was well behind both teams (Renault nearly doubled their points) In fact, they were fighting with one team in an unanticipated outcome: Toyota. Williams 5th, who was in fifth place, appeared unmotivated and BAR-Honda was relegated to sixth.

The year 2006 was the one in which Alonso as well as Renault have been able to renew their title, maintaining their solid knowledge that they had gained from their previous seasons. The battle to win the title was competitive this time. But, the challenge was going to be against Ferrari that appeared to recover from its poor previous season and had hired Massa as a replacement for Barrichello. It turned out to be Fisichella who was in charge of replacing Trulli in Renault.

Motorist.com

McLaren came back to third and was joined by Raikkonen as well as Juan Pablo Montoya (in the first part of championship) along with De la Rosa (second half of the championship) within their squads. The fourth spot was as well for the Japanese team and this time it was Honda.

The tire change were also back and the engines were downgraded to 2.4L V8s instead of 3L V10s.

Chapter 6: 2007 Return Of Ferrari

Ferrari had warned Renault in the previous season about its desire to take back its crown in Formula 1 and made good with its threats during the 2007 season. The development of engines V8 was stopped for 10 seasons in order to reduce costs.

But, it wasn't Michael Schumacher who would bring glory back to the Italian team, since the previous season he declared his retirement and become an Ferrari director advisor. His spot would be filled by Finnish Kimi Raikkonen, known as the "ice person."

The season's final race will be a hotly debated event, with three drivers battling for the title at the final Brazilian Grand Prix. The first of these was double champion Fernando Alonso, who had signed with McLaren in 2007 and was concluding his five-year stint with Renault.

The other driver in the race is a young driver, aged just 22 years old Lewis Hamilton, who shared an partnership alongside Alonso with McLaren and was the first to make his mark with Formula 1. Hamilton would be the British Hamilton would finish second in the championship, with four victories, which would be equal to wins and points to his fellow driver Fernando Alonso. Both would be one point further behind Fernando Alonso, the Finnish champion.

Giantbomb.com

While Between Alonso as well as Hamilton they scored enough points to earn the world title for constructors However, McLaren was not able to win the title. McLaren team was penalized for watching Ferrari which resulted in the cancellation of all points earned during the season , and thus relegating their team into last position. The title will therefore remain with the Italian team, by including Massa's points in the total attained by the champion.

Motor.es

While the battle to win the championship was narrowed to just two teams, Ferrari as well as McLaren, it's worth highlighting the significance that McLaren's BMW Sauber team, second classed after the demise of McLaren and McLaren, and it was the only team that Heidfeld and Kubica were awarded more than 100 points. The United States, Kubica's BMW was driven by Vettel at the time, who was racing with Toro Rosso.

The story of the origins of a new super champion
In 2008, Formula 1 was about to be a major split (with the possibility of establishing an additional championship) due to the struggle of several teams to make ends meet financially. The issue was resolved through an Agreement of Concord that improved the conditions of distribution of earnings for several of Formula 1 teams. This year an unpopular qualification scheme that is based on three rounds is implemented with Q1 as well as Q2 and Q3.
In the previous year in which Lewis Hamilton falling just one point back from the winner on His debut in the championship, it became evident that an upcoming champion was on the way and that eventually the world champion would be crowned. title. What no one could have anticipated was that it would happen that soon, given that in 2007, and through the help of a divine intervention Lewis Hamilton

was able to take the title by just one point over Felipe Massa's Ferrari.

Lat.motorsport.com

However, the incredible ability that is Lewis Hamilton was not enough to allow McLaren to claim the constructors' championship because his teammate Heikki Kovalainen couldn't finish higher than seventh. Alonso was forced to leave the team and returned to Renault and finished fifth in the championship final.

The title for the team is expected to be won by Ferrari With Massa 2nd and Raikkonen third, with an advantage of 21 points over silver bullets.

Pinterest.com

BMW along including Heidfeld and Kubica continued its excellent work and once more became the first team in remaining classes and gaining a dangerously close proximity to McLaren. This proved how in the BMW Williams spinoff the German team did better, while Williams did not perform as well as their best times, finishing eighth place.

Es.wikipedia.org

The infiltration of Brawn The irruption of Brawn

In 2009, during the midst of a scuffle with Ferrari and McLaren-Mercedes new team was formed which was going to break all regulations in Formula 1: Brawn GP.

This season, the KERS was introduced in the race, it is an Energy Recovery System that takes advantage of a portion of the energy lost by the heat generated through the brakes, to convert this into electric energy. This will add power to the motors only a couple of minutes before charging. The motors were operated during three events.

In the current season was a tough one for this season, the Japanese team Toyota and Honda because of their low economic and sporting performance were set to pull out from the tournament. In reality, Toyota would do it at the close of the season in conjunction with BMW.

But, Honda underwent a makeover to become a new team called Brawn GP. The change was not going to be anything but a testimonial.

In the race, with Mercedes engine and Jenson Button as well as Rubens Barrichello as the team's drivers, Brawn won the constructors title, and the title of drivers for the British and showed the superiority of their team that has not been questioned. Except for China the team was able to win six of the initial seven races, thanks largely to the blower exhausts that took advantage of the effect on the ground that was close to rules due to its size.

These exhausts were also employed in Toyota and other teams, as if they wanted to offer extra assistance to teams who were facing the most economic issues. While the other teams made their exhausts based on the Brawn model The results were essentially the same however by the time they were done, the British team already had accumulated many points.

The most impressive performance of Brawn-Mercedes was the age-related 22 Sebastian Vettel, already promoted to the Red Bull first team, which was the best among the other grid and saw Australian Mark Webber finishing fourth. It would be a dramatic and unanticipated increase for the team of energy drinks as the only team capable of competing with Brawn with a final score of just 20 points behind.

Zimbio.com

Hamilton along with Kovalainen's McLaren finished third in the standings, despite an unimpressive performance, which the Briton could squeeze in two victories, while his Finnish teammate was ranked 12th at the top of the table. Ferrari was forced to make use of at least four racers (Massa, Badoer, Fisichella and Raikkonen) lost one point to McLaren.

The golden age of Vettel and Red Bull
Following the controversial Brawn season in the GP and his driver Mercedes purchased more than 75 percent of the team. the German team was reintroduced back to Formula 1 after many years of absence.

It wouldn't be the only one to make a comeback because it was also the case that with the German team, the Seven-time winner Michael Schumacher would return to racing. It was an unknown to determine if Schumacher would be able to come back with the same kind of performance as his glory years.

Additionally, Sauber returned to competition in place of BMW and the previously highly successful Lotus also came back. The world champion Jenson Button, following the demise of Brawn and Brawn, was to be a part of McLaren Mercedes. McLaren Mercedes team with Lewis Hamilton.

So, in the midst of all this changes, there were a lot of in the dirt which Sebastian Vettel quickly began to eliminate, in line with his improvement and success in the previous season. He which would lead to his first world title , and his first title with his Red label Bull (with Renault engines) as a construction firm. Vettel broke the record of a young driver for the title in the world at the age of 23 years and 4 months. The record was which was set just a few months earlier by Lewis Hamilton (23 years and 9 months).

Vettel could become a close champion, as Vettel was just 4 points clear of the second-placed, Fernando Alonso, who in the current season was competing alongside Ferrari.

Australian Mark Webber took third spot at the top of the table, which demonstrates his admiration for Red Bull. Red Bull team and Lewis Hamilton was relegated to fourth. With Button fifth in the standings, Hamilton was fifth. McLaren team had the most to gain from Red Bull's primary rival and Felipe Massa's sixth position resulted in Ferrari be forced be content with third.

Fourth is the new Mercedes team that is enjoying a positive beginning, but not quite the top three teams and with results that are far from their former team as Brawn. Renault is, for their part was able to secure a respectable fifth position after remaining on the field for few months, despite financial issues.

Kaiser's return to Mercedes did not turn out to be what is considered to be a huge success and he finished in seventh place and having nearly half of the points scored by Nico Rosberg, his Mercedes teammate. Nico Rosberg.

The following season would see the same the champions Vettel along with Red Bull taking home their second consecutive title which opened a new era, similar to how it had been occurring during Formula 1 in recent times where teams dominated the stages.

This is despite the fact that an extremely important developments of the past few years in the last few years, the DRS system, A mobile spoiler that makes use on the slipstream flow of the vehicle ahead when it is under a second from it giving an advantage to speed up the ability to overtake. .

This time , the German took the win with more calm and aplomb (with 122 points ahead of Jenson Button's McLaren) which proved that Vettel's talents were growing with age which makes Vettel an unbeatable driver.

The third race was the same Red Bull of Mark Webber and Fernando Alonso could only be fourth behind Ferrari. He was just behind Lewis Hamilton.

At the construction championship this was reflected in Red Bull dominance, with McLaren third, which was well ahead of other teams, but not able to beat the Austrian team of energy drinks.

Third, and also in no-man's-land third would be in the Ferrari consisting of Alonso as well as Massa. Fourth place would be Mercedes (with Schumacher as eighth classified) and the fifth position , it would come Renault this time in the form of Lotus-Renault.

For 2012 however, in spite of the uniqueness of having six championship drivers in the field (Vettel, Alonso, Schumacher, Hamilton, Button and Raikkonen) The results will not be that different. Vettel was able to work along with Red Bull to keep the constructors and drivers title with third place for both.

But the advantage in this race would be diminished and Vettel will have to pay for his third consecutive win. The final decision was not made until the final race of Brazil because Alonso was able to choose between Ferrari and Ferrari however, as he did two years before the Spaniard was forced to settle for second on the podium.

Surprising third position third place for Kimi Raikkonen of the Lotus-Renault. Hamilton along with Button would be in the next spots in the final class as well. Michael Schumacher, 13th and just a few places below co-driver Rosberg in Mercedes was able to decide to quit completely, thus ending his racing career with Formula 1. In the end, he was not able to gain glory back in the German team Seven times world champion was forced to retire.

In terms of the constructors' championship the race was more evenly among Red Bull, Ferrari (2nd classified) and McLaren. However, Renault had a great result by accumulating over 300 points. Mercedes at this point would be in fifth place, just below those of French team.

Does that new level of equality, and cooperation signified this Red Bull era was over? The truth is that during 2013, which was final season for V8 engine, Vettel as well as Red Bull once more won two world championships, the fourth consecutive time for the manufacturer and driver.

Actually rather than the result shrinking, Vettel achieved his fourth title by winning over 150 points in comparison to Alonso who, once again, finished second and was in the shade behind Red Bull and the German driver.

The most noticeable change in the Red Bull era was the increase of Mercedes this year, which although it was unable to match

Ferrari Austrian team, did be able to finish second in the standings by six places ahead of Ferrari.

In this regard, there is many things to consider as well as the disappointing performances by Massa (the the other Ferrari driver) and the decision to sign Mercedes to Lewis Hamilton to replace the recently dismissed Michael Schumacher. Hamilton is fourth in the standings will score the score of 189 points which could be the beginning of an alliance that would be successful in Hamilton's German team.

Curvasenlazadas.com

The other thing that stands out is the calamity for McLaren that, following the death from Lewis as well as having Button along with Sergio Perez at the helm and Sergio Perez in charge, could fall to fifth position, a place lower than those of Renault team (from Grosjean and Raikkonen, with Kovalainen taking part in the final two rounds).

Chapter 7: Hamilton's Reign Mercedes And The Documents Of Hamilton

In 2014, there was the introduction of a new Concord Agreement between the Builders Association and the FIA which gave greater prominence to the teams during negotiations over television rights, 1,600 turbo engines and eight gearboxes were added. gears, meaning that the most suited team would have the advantage of having.

The team that was in question was Mercedes which maintained its growth from the previous season to win back as team at Formula 1. This was due the efforts of Lewis Hamilton, a driver who was definitely the key to revitalizing the Mercedes brand and won his second World Championship.

It is also important to note the new power units featuring energy recovery in the exhaust and braking systems which will mark the next phase of Mercedes as the top motorcyclist from that hybrid and Formula 1 era.

Mercedes dominate was unstoppable and it scored 701 points compared to the Red Bull's 405 points, and ended its dominance with Mercedes practically beating everyone else and winning 16 out of 19 races. In actual fact, Hamilton was first in the standings, with his teammate Rosberg placed second, which is far from third. Mark Webber's Red Bull.

The Williamses due to the Mercedes engines, came in at third spot at the top of the construction championship along with the two drivers Felipe Massa and the Finn Valtteri Bottas in what they claimed was an improvement for this legendary team which was plagued by years of disappointing results.

The team that could go downhill is another of the greatest, McLaren, which would be fifth. Ferrari had an impressive adaptation to the new engines as well, finishing fourth with Alonso sixth, and Raikkonen thirteenth. Both teams are a long way in the distance from Williams, Red Bull, and we have to ask what is the best thing to say about Mercedes.

Following these tense changes in 2015, it was anticipated that teams would have improved their adaptability to the hybrid age. A Virtual Safety Car was also set up, wherein the the event of an accident that was minor or if there was no immediate danger and instead of leaving the Safety Car regrouping the cars the cars, a speed limit was set until the danger was over, while maintaining the distances .

In any event it was clear that the power of Mercedes was even more brutal (again 16 wins out of 19). Mercedes won the championship again as Lewis Hamilton took his third world championship.

It was clear that The German team was also excessive and they scored 703 points in comparison to the 428 in the second class the second class, which was Ferrari with the addition of the four-time winner Sebastian Vettel as Raikkonen's teammate (Alonso joined McLaren). McLaren).

Hamilton and Rosberg were the top two in the standings of drivers ahead of the two Ferrari drivers. Fifth and sixth are those two Williams drivers, Bottas as well as Massa and Massa, respectively. They British team continued to recover and set out to achieve faster times.

Autosport.com

Red Bull was in fourth place (with Ricciardo and Kvyat) in the past, and the times that it was dominant appeared to be a long time ago. McLaren was fifth after dropping Mercedes engines , and in the process joining forces with Honda.

2016 was another season that was dominated by Mercedes Petronas (19 of 21 races) but that was a season in which Lewis Hamilton would give a breathing room to the drivers' title , and be outclassed by his teammate and fellow German Nico Rosberg. Just 5 points separated both drivers, while the title was getting close to its conclusion however the fact that they were dominating the field and having no other drivers to compete with led them to finish second and first in the final race, and a trophy for Rosberg.

Motor.ru

For the other Teams, these were at the back of their respective Formula 1 scene. Red Bull regained at least second on the championship for constructors and that was aided by the rise of a gifted Max Verstappen. even if Well was racing behind his teammate Ricciardo and was already looking for ways towards becoming the fastest driver ever to win a race in the

Spanish Grand Prix (18 years 7 months, fifteen days).

The third place was taken by third was the Ferrari team, which was a considerable difference of Red Bull, and far in the back came Williams and Force India. Force India and Williams teams featuring Mercedes engines. The partnership that was formed between McLaren and Honda didn't produce results however, and the British team was left in sixth place.

In 2017, the champion Nico Rosberg was retiring citing the pressure of competition and that his place at Mercedes was taken by ValtteriBottas. The Finn despite his excellent work, was not able enough to take on Lewis Hamilton who won his fourth world title, and third in succession for the Mercedes team which, was able to easily surpass the competition, even though at Ferrari did manage to compete against Vettel and Raikkonen. This reduced Mercedes winnings by a mere five compared with 12 in those of the Italian team.

Red Bull was third again which was far ahead of Ferrari and its rivals and Max Verstappen getting close to Ricciardo.

Force India, with the Mexican Sergio Perez and the French Esteban Ocon, will make up the team to continue the excellent performance that is the Indian team.

In the case of the historic teams, Williams would have to be content with fifth place, and McLaren would start to suffer for the bad decision to feed off Honda engines, slipping to ninth position and the last team which could only surpass Sauber in the midst of a season-long that was a disaster.

The 2018 season is not going to be too different, with the fight with Mercedes and Ferrari and Ferrari, but with a an impressive advantage for Ferrari's German team (11 wins against six). The main fight will take place one between Hamilton and Vettel winning for Hamilton. The British Vettel bringing his fifth title to his personal collection.

It is important to note that due to the strength of Mercedes and the Mercedes team, if anyone could add excitement to the title it was his teammate Bottas who failed to have a win throughout the entire season.

Essentiallysports.com

In this fight, which was two-colored (if it qualifies as an actual fight) Max Verstappen was the top fighter of Red Bull beating Ricciardo and placing himself over Bottas, sneaking in between Ferraris as well as Mercedes.

So, Mercedes, Ferrari and Red Bull would be the three first to be classified for the construction championships as prior to the season. The biggest surprises would be found below. Renault was fourth position and was being followed by Haas which is an American team that been in existence since 2016 but whose car was regarded as a replica of Ferrari.

F1experiences.com

McLaren continued to struggle but now using Renault engines, it could be able to at the very least regain the sixth position and then move from the last places. The drama would unfold this time around for Williams and he would get past the final spot with the elimination of Force India, which would be back the following year in the form of Racing Point with the purchase of the team by Lawrence Stroll, father of the team's pilot Lance Stroll.

2019 will be another year of totality and continues for Mercedes and has seen 15 victories. Three wins of Max Verstappen for Red Bull and three for Ferrari and one in the name of Vettel as well as two wins for Charles Leclerc, escaped him.

Concerning the internal workings of Mercedes while Bottas did win four wins however, he wasn't as successful as Hamilton's 11 wins, in what is a cosy teammate for Hamilton. Briton as well as to the Mercedes team which is able to avoid significant competition conflicts.

This isn't an ideal situation for the viewers. In a time that only one Mercedes can be able to compete against another Mercedes and we are not able to enjoy the thrill of a intense battle between the two drivers.

It is worth mentioning the first appearance of Formula 1 of Leclerc, the driver who was destined for amazing things. Not just due to Leclerc's record for being the youngest person to be able to win successive races (at 21 years 10 months, 21 days) as well as due to his character and performance in the driving arena, surpassing an all-time champion in the form of Sebastian Vettel in his first season. Tired of Ferrari's inability to keep up with Mercedes. Leclerc has become the dream to see the next chapter of a return to Ferrari's Italian team.

In 2019 Mercedes once again won an impressive win and the Ferrari second-placed team and looking more into the rearview mirror as it tries to maintain its second position in the battle against Red Bull than trying to surpass the all-powerful German team.

Max Verstappen is the first recognized driver in the class ahead of the other two Mercedes and in more mature manner as compared to this Dutch driver with the talent to spare to commemorate an time. It is because of his talent which Red Bull is unable to find a rival to matchit, and has relegated Pierre Gasly to his secondary team Toro Rosso this season and switching the team's Toro Rosso towards Thai Alexander Albon.

The irruption of coronavirus in Formula 1
2020 was set to be another year of change without any major modifications. Conscient of the boredom and monotony caused by

the superiority of Mercedes was causing the fans for a long time and deprived them of any excitement and viewing every race as a repeat of the last one, and being a German teams always winning, a new policy was put in place for 2021.

The regulation, which was enacted with the intention of adjusting budgets in order to cut expenses, was enacted to ensure that teams were balanced by imposing spending limitations, to make them equal in terms of economic amounts so that it could translate into an equal track. Formula 1 knows how important it is to maintain the fan base, especially with the diversity of entertainment on pay-TV. This requires greater equality in the race as well as more fights and less monotony and predictability.

The new regulations will also bring an end to the flat bottom, and be more flexible with the ground effect, which would facilitate taking overtakes since aerodynamics aren't affected by the slipstream, which allows the car to remain further away from the vehicle in front which will increase the amount of overtakes that can be made among the major actions during the program.

The coronavirus pandemic was discovered which shattered strategies to enter Formula 1 and affecting the race and the sport as a whole. The championship was in limbo and the vehicle development at a standstill the new rules were delayed until 2022.

It meant Formula 1's Formula 1 revolution would have to wait another year to see what it could bring and it was not just that, but also 2020 and 2021 were anticipated to mirror the race that was seen in the past on the track with the same cars with limited modifications to cut costs due to the loss of pandemics.

Overall the team assumed that in 2020 the only thing to alter the Mercedes was its color (with the black color in protest to an Anti-Racist Blacks live matter campaign). In the 13th race and with four races left to be completed in the championship Mercedes took home the constructors' title at Imola which was the seventh time in a row , since 2014.

One of the lingering questions was the possibility that Lewis Hamilton would win his seventh world championship, which would tie Michael Schumacher as the two drivers to have won the most world championships. Bottas was not able to resist, like in previous years as did Lewis Hamilton was crowned drivers champion in Turkey only the same race that his team had won the title. The Briton was a legend by winning seven times and thus equalled the record-setting number of Kaiser championships.

In 2021, which had an overall championship that had very similar features to the previous year, but without significant modifications, it was anticipated that Mercedes will continue to be the dominant team and that Hamilton would not have any trouble in beating Michael Schumacher's record for championships. However the two teams, Lewis and Mercedes faced a significant obstacle in the form of Max Verstappen as well as Red Bull.

The team of energy drinks was awestruck by its performance at the start of the season. They had the single-seater racer being extremely competitive, exceeding and even catching Mercedes as well as Verstappen having won five out of the initial nine races, and Hamilton winning four races.

The resulting equality created a fierce racing and a rivalry likes of which have never been seen on the track in several years. Both drivers fought each other on the course to the end without a smidgen of restraint and so ferociously that the rules regarding what is legal for certain kinds of overtaking was tested with many people complaining they are too restricting.

The rivalry was at its height at Silverstone in the form of Hamilton hitting his front wheel against the back of the Verstappen's Red Bull causing him to fall heavily. The Briton did not suffer any penalty and this increased the ferocity of the battle both on both sides of the tracks. At Monza it was Verstappen's vehicle that landed over Hamilton's Mercedes and could cause more damage had not been due to the Halo.

Desporto.sapo.pt

The two drivers enter the final race with identical points, in one of the most thrilling races ever in Formula 1 history. With Verstappen in pole position but he was unable to hold pole in the beginning but

Hamilton used the opportunity to get away from him during the entire race.

In the final laps it was difficult for Verstappen and Hamilton to keep pace and Hamilton could be celebrating his eighth title in the world championship. An accident involving Latifi's Williams resulted in the removal of a safety car which ended any gap that existed that existed between Hamilton as well as Verstappen. Safety cars were removed just one lap later which caused the championship to be decided on one lap, for the very first time in the history of racing. Verstappen was pitting with newer and more efficient tires, seized this chance to win, and beat Hamilton and took the win to become the world champion to the very first time in his professional career.

The Dutchman took the driver's championship for Red Bull in an unexpected manner, however the constructors title was awarded to Mercedes that retained its lead in the hybrid era . It also took home the 8th title for the company.

In 2022, the revolutionary phase of the rules will be in place that will transform Formula 1 upside down. Strangely the new rules, designed to create equality in the sport that had been boring for a number of years, will be introduced following an extremely evenly and thrilling seasons ever.

How will this affect the teams? The question remains determined what the impact will be on teams. Mercedes can remain dominant, despite its undisputed hegemony in period of the hybrid engine. It is also unclear if Red Bull, now that appears to be catching up to the German manufacturer and will be in a position to keep its leadership performance, particularly following the expiration of its contract with Honda as the engine manufacturer.

In the end, the problem is how Ferrari will ever and for all be able to compete on the same level as the other main competitors. After another year of being far from Mercedes as well as Red Bull, and even occasionally McLaren, the famous Italian constructor made a positive growth throughout the year to finish in third place however it is yet to be determined what the future holds for the Italian constructor. is favorable for it to restore its fame and fight to win the title of world champion. The two drivers of the team, Leclerc and Carlos Sainz have shown a tremendous potential that will bring their fans lots of enjoyment should they be able to create a single-seater that is competitive.

Todonoticia.cl

For McLaren In 2021, it took a different path to Ferrari. It began with a great performance, and was the third best team for portion of championship however, its decline in the final stretch resulted in it finishing in fourth position, way from its previous glory however, it improved its performance in the last bad years, and with the addition of a Norris that showed a remarkable improvement even though Ricciardo did not perform at the level that was expected of him.

One step back was Renault who was rebranded as of Alpine and their return Fernando Alonso to the team which saw him achieve his greatest accomplishments. Although the results were comparable to the previous seasons for the builder however, the addition of Alonso has brought optimism to the team that is optimistic about an excellent future. Along with the progress of Esteban Ocon who scored his first victory on the track in Formula 1.

Thebestf1.es

The team behind Renault was AlphaTauri which was the Red Bull subsidiary team, which was sometimes at a higher echelon, performing as the third-best car, with Gasly at his highest level returning back to Red Bull and a rookie Yuki Tsunoda stepping up his first steps into the contest.

Formula1.lne.es

In terms of Aston Martin's first performance as a team, and as the successor of Racing Point, more was expected from the performance which was average and did not provide many opportunities to a more settled Sebastian Vettel and a Lance Stroll who appears to have attained his maximum capabilities as a driver in Formula 1.

Posterlounge.es

For Williams however, even though it saw some improvement after the arrival of investors from other countries however, it did not have any aspirations beyond not reaching the final positions, with a fantastic Russell who was able to secure his seat at

Mercedes in 2021. He also secured the Latifi without many options during the time that Claire Williams retired from management and her father Frank Williams, founder of the team and a racing legend passed away.

Graining.es

Alfa Romeo finished second to last in the standings in the year when Kimi Raikkonen quit racing after 21 years of Formula 1, 21 victories and one world championship. Teammate Giovinazzi did not deliver the promised performance and ended his partnership with the team too.

Motor.es

The American Haas team finished the class, using the car that had previously stated that it will not be upgraded or modified due to financial issues, and it also gave the team's two newcomers in the competition: Mick Schumacher, the son of the seven-time champion who proved superior over his teammate, the Russian Nikita Mazepin with no options to compete effectively in the weakest vehicle that is on the grid.

Thebestf1.es

All of this an additional season in the long and storied race of Formula 1 comes to an endin 2022. Then, in 2022, the sport will begin the new chapter by introducing a revolutionary regulations , which will bring different single-seaters in comparison to the current ones.

Are there real-time changes in the contest or will the trends of previous years persist? We'll only know an answer when the engines begin to roar as they open the new chapter in the story of this enthralling contest.

Annexed
Drivers with the highest number of titles
Pilot Titles Years
Michael Schumacher 7 1994, 1995 2000, 2001 2002, 2003, 2004,
Lewis Hamilton 7 2008, 2014, 2015and 2017, 2018 and 2019 2020
Juan Manuel Fangio 5 1951, 1954, 1955, 1956, 1957
Sebastian Vettel 4 2010, 2011, 2012, 2013
Alain Prost 4 1985, 1986 1989, 1993,
Jack Brabham 3 1959, 1960 1965,
Jackie Stewart 3 1969, 1971, 1973
Niki Lauda 3 , 1975, and 1984
Nelson Piquet 3 1981, 1983, 1987

Ayrton Senna 3 1988, 1990, 1991
Alberto Ascari 2 1952, 1953
Jim Clark 2 1963, 1965
Graham Hill 2 1962, 1968
Emerson Fittipaldi 2 1972, 1974
Mika Hakkinen 2 1998, 1999
Fernando Alonso 2 2005, 2006
Giuseppe Farina 1 1950
Mike Hawthorn 1 1958
Phil Hill 1 1961
John Surtees 1 1964
Denny Hulme 1 1967
Jochen Rindt 1 1970
James Hunt 1 1976
Mario Andretti 1 1978
Jody Scheckter 1 1979
Alan Jones 1 1980
Keke Rosberg 1 1982
Nigel Mansell 1 1992
Damon Hill 1 1996
Jacques Villeneuve 1 1997
Kimi Raikkonen 1 2007
Jenson Button 1st of 2009
Nico Rosberg 1 2016

Max Verstappen
1

2021

Annexed
Builders with additional titles
Builder Titles Years
Ferrari 16 1961 1964, 1975 1976 1977, 1979, 1982 1984, 1998, 2000 2001, 2002, 2003 2004 and 2007. 2008
Williams 9 1980 1981, 1986, 1987 1992, 1993 1994 1996, 1997
Mclaren 8 1974, 1984, 1985, 1988, 1989, 1990, 1991, 1998
Mercedes 8 2014, 2015, and 2016 2017, 2018 2019 2020, 2021,
Lotus 7 1963 1965, 1968 1970 1972 1973 1978
Red Bull 4 2010, 2011, 2012, 2013,
Cooper 2 1959, 1960
Brabham 266 and 1967
Renault 2 2005, 2006
Vanwall 1 1958
Benetton 1. Nineteen-Ninety Five
BRM 1 1962
Matra 1 1969
Tyrrell 1st, 1971
Brawn 1 2009

Britain

In 1950 The International Automobile Federation managed to bring together six of the biggest grand prizes in the same regulations (plus that of the Indianapolis 500 as a scoring event) in order to create the first season that was officially known as the Formula One Drivers World Championship. It was a race for vehicles equipped with 4.5 Liter naturally aspirated and 1.5 supercharged engine. The contest started on May 13, 1950, at the Silverstone circuit in Great Britain.

In the past, a European championship was established, but it was interrupted because of during the Second World War. After the war was concluded and following the restructuring of the FIA the team could begin the very first race of the inaugural year of the championship which was to become the legend that is now Formula 1.

In the first edition, only the five most skilled drivers took home points, which was divided into 8, 6, 4 3, 2 and 1 points. There was also an extra score for the best lap. The only criteria was the four top results from all season's races for every driver and in the event that they were sharing the same car in one race points were divided equally among each.

The first pole in the championship was awarded to Italian Giuseppe Farina, aboard the supercharged Alfa Romeo 148, a post-war automobile that was built in 1938, which issued its first warning during the initial classification.

[1]

Alongside Farina, Alfa Romeo took the top four spots on the first row of the starting grid, alongside Luigi Fagioli, Juan Manuel Fangio and Reg Parnell.

The advantage in the performance of Alfa Romeo was also demonstrated during the race, when the top three positions were filled by drivers of the Italian brand who are part of their Alfa Romeo SpA team. Only one did not finish at top of the race and it was Fangio who had to pull out because of engine issues caused by a ruptured oil tube.

In the race of Alfa Romeo drivers, it was Farina who was also the one to win the race and claimed the first win to win in Formula 1 history. Although he led for the majority of the race but he was also engaged in a

close fight with teammate Fagioli until the final.
[2]
A British Reg Parnell accompanied his teammates on the podium, though far away from them following a collision with a hare at the time of the race.

The top two scoring positions came to drivers from the French Automobiles Talbot-Darracq team, with Yves Giraud -Cabantous in fourth place and Louis Rosier fifth.

Two laps were a bit behind those who led, and proved that the performance of Alfa Romeos was superior since the beginning of the championship.

Monaco

Then, in Monaco, Scuderia Ferrari made its debut, but the main role remained to be held by Alfa Romeo, with Fangio at the top of the podium and Farina placing second. At at least Jose Froilan Gonzales's Maserati did manage to make it to the first row, so that it wouldn't be held by Alfa Romeo again.

The race was decided by a wave from the sea that swept over the port, encroaching on the track along the curve of Tabac. Nino Farina attempted to stay clear of her , but she caused an accident that impacted his competitors (up up to eight required a retreat).

Fangio was capable of removing this confusion and emerge to win the race, which was won comfortably by a lap ahead of Alberto Ascari's Ferrari and Raymmond Summer's fourth-place finish was a solid start to fans of the Italian team.

[3]

Indianapolis 500

The third race of the inaugural season was the famous Indianapolis 500 race, the only race that was not European in the inaugural season of the World Cup, and in this instance, and even up to 1960, was scoring in the race.

The European teams did not participate because of the expense of transporting their machines and vehicles to America. United States, so it had no major effect on World Cup beyond the fact that Johnnie Parsons, winner of the test, was equal to the top two scorers by 9 points Giuseppe Farina and Juan Manuel Fangio.

While he didn't take part in a championship race yet however, he was able to be 6th in his final standings.
[4]
Swiss
On Bremgarten, on the Bremgarten circuit, there was a return to normal to the racing where all three Alfa Romeos again demonstrated their dominance with Fangio the winner and Fagioli taking pole. Farina and Fagioli finishing third and second.

The team was without Jose Froilan Gonzalez off the grid due to burns sustained from the crash that he had in Monaco Alfa Romeo's biggest competitors included Ferrari racers Luigi Villoresi and Alberto Ascari who finished in fourth and fifth place.

Fangio began leading the race until lap seven , he was outpaced by teammate Farina. The two Ferraris were fighting with the Fagioli's Alfa Romeo... until they finally were forced to pull out from the race, as did Villoresi because of engine issues, and Ascari because of an oil leak.

Fangio was forced to withdraw because of engine issues which led to Farina's victory.
[5]

Fagioli was second, atop Farina in the top spot. Third spot was awarded to Frenchman Louis Rosier who got the first podium of Talbot-Lago.

Half the championship was completed, Nino Farina led the world championship with 18 points. He was being followed by Luigi Fagioli with 12 and Fangio with 9th fourth place.

Belgium

Five races of the season took place at Spa-Francorchamps and, as usual, all three Alfa Romeos claimed the top spots in the race With Nino Farina leading Fangio as well as Fagioli.

The Alphas led the race in the first part of the race. However, when the fuel stops Frenchman Raymond Sommer began leading the race in his Talbot... until his engine failed.

The main role was given back to Alfa Romeos in which Juan Manuel Fangio managed to take the win ahead of Fagioli. Louis Rosier, once again joined his two Alfa athletes on top of the podium after taking over Farina who was struggling with transmission issues.

[6]
With two races left Fagioli's win has tightened the race: Farina was the leader with 22 points. Fagioli second with 18 as well as third was the Argentine fourth with 17 points.

France

The final race in the series held in Reims-Gueux. after the Ferraris disbanding The Alfa Romeos had no rivals and were able to climb back up to top position in the rankings which culminated in Fangio winning the third time he has topped poles in just six races.

But it was Farina who led the initial race of the French race, and then problems with fuel forced him to last place. He attempted to regain his position and eventually climbed to seventh.

The battle for victory was refocused on Fangio and Fagioli The Argentine was the winner and added an additional win Fagioli was left in the second spot.

Third was British Peter Whitehead, who was only three laps away from Fagioli in the private Ferrari. In the aftermath of the

French race, and only one more race to win the championship Fangio took the lead of the championship by scoring 26 points. This was in contrast to 24 points for Fagioli in addition to 22 from Farina and Farina in an exciting final.

Italy

Monza was the race which decided the first year of Fomula 1. Fangio was able to be either first or second to be champion, regardless of how his teammates performed. Farina required to finish third, and Fagioli is the only one that was more difficult: he had to win, run the fastest time, ensure that Farina was not able to finish higher than third and that Fangio didn't get a score.

Fangio won pole position during a qualifying session, where Ascari was second over all of the Alfa Romeo drivers.

Farina was the leader of the first stages of the race along with Fangio and Ascari extremely close to him till the Ferrari driver had to pull out because of overheating the engine. The race was left to the win for Farina as well as Fangio ... up to just two laps later, the Argentine was forced to stop because of gearbox issues. The Argentine was then able to get on the Piero Taruffi's Alfa Romeo 150, hoping to earn a share of points which would enable him to win the title however, he was forced to pull out because of engine issues.

It was Italian Nino Farina successful in winning the race that made him a world champion. He became the first driver to win to ever win in Formula 1.

[8]

Final CLASSIFICATION 1950
(Drivers who earned points)
Giuseppe Farina 30
Juan Manuel Fangio 27
Luigi Fagioli 24
Louis Rosier 13
Alberto Ascari 11
Johnnie Parsons 9
Bill Holland 6
Prince Bira 5 Bira 5
Peter Whitehead 4
Louis Chiron 4
Reg Parnell 4
Mauri Rose 4
Dorino Serafini 3

3
Raymond Sommer 3
Cecil Green 3
Robert Manzon 3
Philippe Etancelin 3
Felice Bonetto 2
Jole Chitwood 1
Tony Bettenhausen 1
Eugene Chaboud 1

1951
Swiss

In 1951, there were eight scoring races in this championship in the world, with the first of which was the Swiss Grand Prix. Alfa Romeo was the favorite manufacturer due to its impressive performance in the previous year, however Ferrari that had racked up at least four wins in races prior to the championship, positioned itself as a real threat.

On the Bremgarten circuit at Bremgarten, the four Alfa Romeos have taken it upon themselves to take all top positions on the list, increasing their lead over the previous season and only Luigi Villoresi's Ferrari being in third place. Juan Manuel Fangio, Nino

Farina, Consalvo Sanesi and Toulo de Graffenried took the positions between the top five spots.

The race began in the rain , on a circuit that was dangerous because of the number of trees that surround the circuit. The race's main competitors of the race were Fangio, Farina and Piero Taruffi, all of them with Ferrari. Nino Farina opted to adopt the no-stop method to change tires. This proved to be a bad decision and allowed his teammate Fangio to take the win with an Alfa Romeo 159 and Taruffi finished second, which is an impressive outcome for Ferrari.

[9]

Indianapolis 500

The second scoring race of this year's world championship was again the famous Indianapolis 500, just 3 days following the race in Switzerland. This is why the major teams participating in the race were not present due to the time and logistical challenges of participating as well as the absence of a European participant.

The race concluded in victory for Lee Wallard with Kurtis-Kraft Offenhauser without repercussions for the race.

Belgium

The race returned to its normal pace with the fastest circuit in the calendar, Spa-Francorchamps, which spans over 14 km. Fangio won pole position, and was followed by teammate Nino Farina. Third and fourth in the class included Luigi Villoresi, Alberto Ascari and Piero Taruffi. This proved that Ferrari did not intend to ease the burden for Alfa Romeo in a race with a dangers, only 13 competitors were registered.

Fangio was having issues with his wheel He finished his race on the ninth So the battle for the win came down to Farina along with the 2 Ferrari drivers. It was the Italian Alfa Romeo took the victory as did Ascari as well as Villoresi completed the podium.

France

The race was dubbed the European Grand Prix, the fourth race took place on the French circuit of Reims-Gueux. Again it was the Alfa Romeo of Fangio and Farina took the top two places then being followed by Ferraris of Villoresi and Ascari.

In the course, Fangio had mechanical problems and Ascari had a gearbox issue. Ascari continued to race his own Ferrari that his fellow teammate Jose Froilan Gonzalez, while Fangio was able to do the same with his Alfa Romeo of his teammate Luigi Fagioli. Following this switch both returned to the lead of the race, and the final win going to Fangio because Ascari also suffered brake issues.

[10]

Nino Farina also ran into issues with his car, but he ended up finishing fifth after that of the Ferraris from Luigi Villoresi, who completed the podium, and British Reg Parnell.

In the final stage of this championship race, which was the longest in the history the championship at 610 kilometers, Fangio led the competition by scoring 15 points. He was followed by his co-teammate Farina just a bit behind at 14 points.

Luigi Fagioli, out of frustration over having to surrender the car he owned to Fangio He decided to take a break soon from racing and ended in a fatal crash during a race for sports cars in Monaco the next year.

[11]

Britain

Following the opening half of the championship racing was on at Silverstone in which Argentine Jose Froilan Gonzales's pole for Ferrari was a surprise to him.

In the race during the race, it was the 1.5 hypercharged Alfa Romeo was still the fastest car on the track however it was also the biggest energy-intensive. This caused Fangio as well as Farina to to stop for refueling twice.

Instead the Ferrari's 4.5L naturally-aspirated V12 engine was able to allow Jose Froilan Gonzalez to finish the race only once, giving him an advantage that allowed him to take victory. He also won the grand prize in the history of racing for being the first race to be won. by Ferrari.

[12]

Fangio was second, while Farina was third. This enabled the Argentine to gain 6 points ahead in the race in the particular race against those Alfa Romeo drivers.

Germany

In 1952, sports events were once again permitted to take place in West Germany, allowing the German Grand Prix to return in 1939. It was held on the treacherous

Nurburgring Nordschleife, also known as the 22.8-kilometer "green hell".

Ascari won pole position as did his co-pilot Jose Froilan Gonzalez, which proved the growing power of Ferrari that already poses a threat to that of the Alfa Romeo of Fangio and Farina which was lagging behind in qualifying.

Farina was able to secure the top spot, but later she had to withdraw due to heat exhaustion. Fangio also experienced mechanical issues and was unable to operate his first and second gear in the car's four.

However, the Argentine continued to race however Ascari was able to catch his rival after the pit stop and claimed the victory in the second race for Ferrari.

[13]

Fangio was the second place finisher in the race, followed by three additional Ferraris including Jose Froilan, Luigi Villoresi and Piero Taruffi. This is a clear upswing to this Italian manufacturer.

Farina's departure resulted in Ascari to climb to second place at the top of the

Championship standings. just 10 points ahead of Fangio and with just two races left.
Italy

In the penultimate race of the championship, held at Monza, Alfa Romeo regained its position as the top team with pole, and one more, and a third place from Fangio and second position in the standings behind Farina.

In the race the Alfa Romeos once again were unable to maintain their reliability. Both of them had to pull out however Farina was able to keep going in Felice Bonetto's car. They managed to finish third and was unable to avoid the double victory of Ascari as well as Jose Froilan Gonzalez with the Ferrari 375, in a race that began by a dominance for Alfa but every time it delivered more wins to Ferrari.

[14]

This also equalized the standings for championship. In spite of mechanical problems, Fangio held the lead however, he was only two points clear of Ascari. Four points back as The Ferrari that was driven by Jose Froilan Gonzalez was third.
Spain

The last day of the championships, at the Pedralbes street circuit in Barcelona ended the course of a year that had been slowly equalizing itself. Fangio scored two points clear of Ascai However, Ferrari was in top form.

Pole was a finalist at Ascari and finished ahead of Fangio In the most obvious indication of his potential to compete with his rival for the title. The third place finisher came Jose Froilan Gonzalez, also with the possibility of being champion.

Jose Froilan Gonzalez lost several spots at the beginning of the season which hampered his chances of winning the final. However, Fangio managed to reach the top spot towards winning and the title.

Alongside the excellent performances of Argentine, Ferrari had opted for a smaller wheel than normal in a move that was not to be correct and, by the time they rectified their mistake Ascari had already been two laps ahead of the Argentine.

This is how Fangio Argentine Juan Manuel Fangio managed to win the race, and this was his first ever world championship.

[15]

Alberto Ascari was finally runner-up at the championship, with Jose Froilan Gonzalez third. Nino Farina was unable to win the title, was third in the last class.

Final CLASSIFICATION 1951
(Drivers who earned points)
Juan Manuel Fangio 31
Alberto Ascari 25
Jose Froilan Gonzalez 24
Nino Farina 19
Luigi Villoresi 15
Piero Taruffi 10
Lee Walland 9
Felice Bonetto 7
Mike Nazaruk 6
Reg Parnell 5
Luigi Fagioli 4
Consalvo Sanesi 3
Louis Rosier 3
Andy Linden 3
Manny Ayuto 2
Jack McGrath 2
Toulo de Graffenried 2
Yves Giraud-Cabantous 2
Bobby Ball 2

1952
Swiss

The decision to pull out of 1952's Alfa Romeo was surprising. Despite winning the championship in the initial two years of contest, the decision from the Italian government to fund the building project forced the company to leave despite the accomplishments.

This caused Ferrari almost without competition, and also stifled the possibility of an opportunity to fight again between the two manufacturers. The FIA has decided to introduce Formula 2 regulations this year to make it mandatory for Ferrari to change its engine, and also allow access to additional manufacturers.

Nino Farina, not able to sign a contract was signed by Ferrari and Fangio was injured in an accident that was fatal in Monza prior to the start of the race and was unable to take part all season.

In addition, during the inaugural race held in Switzerland Ferrari's top drivers weren't available because Ascari was in preparation to race in his race at the Indianapolis 500 and Luigi Villoresi was also involved in an accident.

This is why the season kicked off with a pole race for Nino Farina's Ferrari which was then and then his colleague Piero Taruffi. Frenchman Robert Manzon slipped into third position in the standings, ahead by those Ferraris from Andre Simon and Rudi Fischer.

Nino Farina was the leader of in the final race, but was forced to stop because of mechanical issues. He tried to stay using Andre Simon's Ferrari however, an issue with the engine forced him to retire.

This enabled Italian Piero Taruffi to win easily, well ahead of his colleague Rudi Fischer.

[16]

The podium was complete with Frenchman Jean Behra with the Gordini who was crowned the most skilled constructor after Ferrari.

Indianapolis 500

As is the norm there was no sign of any team took part in this year's North American test, except for Alberto Ascari who participated with Ferrari but had to withdraw after 40 laps in an event that was ultimately won by Troy Ruttman and another year that did not have a huge influence on Formula 1 world championship.

Belgium

Ascari made his return to Spa-Francorchamps to win the championship with pole as well as the fastest lap. In this manner Ascari posed a threat to the Italian driver vowed to assert his dominance on the race.

[17]

Nino Farina came in second place to complete the Ferrari double. The podium was complete with Robert Manzon, achieving a record-breaking win in the Equipe Gordini which stood out from all the other competitors, yet not as impressive as Ferrari. In reality, Jean Behra had managed to win the race right from the beginning.

France

At the Rouen track The dominance of Ferrari continued unabated With Ascari, Farina and Taruffi making it to the top three spots ahead of Gordini de Behra , and Manzon.

Alberto Ascari also continued to dominating the race from beginning to end and claimed another win.

[18]

Farina was second, as did Taruffi came third who achieved the Ferrari triple. In the background, Frenchman Robert Manzon was fourth for Gordini.

Britain

At the British race, Ferrari continued to enjoy their season in complete peace, however this time, it was Nino Farina who won the pole, attempting to disrupt Ascari's supreme dominance.

But, a malfunction caused by the spark plugs ruined Farina's racing career. She finished ninth in the race, not able to sustain her battle with Ascari who won the win, finishing fifth in a row, and prolonging the streak of victories.

[19]

Piero Taruffi was second, however, the podium this time was not topped by Gordini however, it was achieved the podium was topped by Mike Hawthorn with Cooper. In fact, it was an excellent race for British drivers and their drivers, such as Dennis

Porce was fourth and Eric Thompson fifth, both together with Connaught.

Germany

At the Nurburgring-Nordschleife circuit the championship continued its usual trend, with Alberto Ascari taking pole and turning it into yet another victory. Ascari continued to turn every race of his season into wins and the one of Germany has earned him the honour of being declared world champion, with two races to be decided.

[20]

Nino Farina came in second and Rudi Fischer made the Ferrari triple, which was followed by Taruffi fourth. Following them, again, it was Jean Behra with Gordini.

Holland

With the championship already decided, Luigi Villoresi returned to the contest after recoveringand replaced Piero Taruffi. Ascari already champion was not content and won the first place before Farina.

Mike Hawthorn took third position on the grid for the start, along with Cooper over Luigi Villorersi, and he shined against the Ferraris during the opening stages of the race. However, the Italian team took over again on Zandvoort. Zandvoort circuit.

Ascari returned to claim another victory , completing the hat-trick of Ferrari With Farina third as well as Villoresi third. Hawthorn was fourth.

[21]

Italy

The season came to an end with Monza in Italy, where Scuderia Ferrari was able to commemorate its amazing year. Alberto Ascari returned to achieve the position of pole and set the goal of winning all races where he was a participant.

But, during the race there was a surprise competitor in the form of Argentine Jose Froilan Gonzalez who was racing for Maserati who was delayed in the race. The Argentine took the lead in the beginning of the race. However, the pit stop was very slow and eliminated his chances of winning but he did recover to finish in second place ahead by Villoresi as well as Farina. This gives hope that Maserati might challenge for the title in the next season, particularly in the event of an appearance by Fangio.

In the meantime, a highly successful season was drawing to a close for Ferrari that had taken Ascari to the title and also led Nino Farina, as well as Piero Taruffi to third and second places respectively.

Final CLASSIFICATION 1952
(Drivers who earned points)
Alberto Ascari 36
Nino Farina 24
Piero Taruffi 22
Rudi Fischer 10
Mike Hawthorn 10
Robert Manzon 9
Troy Ruttman 8
Luigi Villoresi 8
Jose Froilan Gonzalez 6.5
Jim Rathmann 6
Jean Behra 6
Sam Hanks 4
Ken Wharton 3
Dennis Poore 3
Duane Carter 3
Alan Brown 2
Maurice Trintignant 2
Paul Frere 2
Felice Bonetto 2

Art Cross 2
Eric Thompson 2
Bill Vukovich 1

1953
Argentina
In 1953, the World Cup began in Argentina The first test of the tournament outside of Europe in case it is not the Indianapolis 500 is not taken into consideration. Again, using Formula 2 rules.

Scuderia Ferrari was once again the most likely to take home a new title with current champion Ascari as the principal driver. However, the return to Fangio as a driver for Maserati could create a huge problem for Ferrari.

Fangio did not have luck in his home country, having to go home due to a malfunctioning transmission. The first Maserati to finish the race came in third-placed car of Jose Froilan Gonzalez.

The winner was Alberto Ascari, who extended his winning streak in front of his co-teammate Luigi Villoresi, getting the first Ferrari double of the season. On the other hand, Mike Hawthorn, who had signed with the Italian team following his successful performance with Cooper was fourth.

The race would remain in the memory for the crash caused by Nino Farina. The Italian was an exit from the corner in which it struck a part of the crowd that was not properly positioned which resulted in the deaths of nine spectators as well as numerous injuries.

[22]

Indianapolis 500

There was a further edition in which there was no mention in Formula 1 in the Formula 1 championship in the North American test that resulted in a win for Bill Vukovich and that had no connection to the contest.

Holland

In Zandvoort, Ascari took pole and was followed by Fangio In what could be the beginning of the much-anticipated fight against Ferrari as well as Maserati.

But the "crooked" was unable to fix the axle after 36 laps , and Fangio was forced to quit to re-enter the race for the third time.

The battle for the victory then was in the hands of Ascari And Nino Farina. Alberto Ascari emerged victorious in the Ferrari

driver's duel winning another one to his record of never losing.
[23]
Third place went to Jose Froilan Gonzalez, who after breaking the axle of his Maserati was able to take the car that belonged to his co-teammate Felice Bonetto and climbed to the top of the podium.

Belgium

As Ascari and Ferrari winning due to Maserati's constant issues with reliability and the race was moved to Belgium for the fourth time in. Juan Manuel Fangio got pole and Ascari was forced be content with second place on a circuit that saw Maserati set records for speed and the attendance record was 100,000.

The Maseratis were ahead in the beginning of the race The Maseratis were ahead, with Jose Froilan Gonzalez leading ahead of Fangio... until both suffered engine failures leading to retirement and leaving Ascari in the top spot over Farina. Ascari ultimately won the race using the help of his Ferrari 500 and Farina's retirement due to engine failure, earned Hawthorn second place.
[24]

Third was Argentine Onofre Marmon who debuted alongside Maserati and displayed the improvement in the company's performance.

France

In Reims in Reims, the equality between Ferrari and Maserati was already a fact that would eventually lead to an event that would be among the top infamous racing events in the history of Formula 1. Ascari was the first to take pole position, along with Ferrari and Maserati taking part in the class.

The equality between builders was reflected through a spirited battle among Fangio as well as Mike Hawthorn. The fight lasted for sixty laps, with both teams swapping the lead several times (practically on every corner of the track there was an overtaking battle between the two).

Two laps later and they both finished in tandem the race was won by Briton who took home his first race by just one second advantage over Fangio.

[25]

Additionally, Jose Froilan Gonzalez finished third, only 4 tenths slower than Fangio And

Ascari finished fourth place, with a time of 3 seconds. So, between the top four ranked there was only five seconds difference. This was an incredible feat for the time, and even after 500 km, meaning that the race was later referred to as "The race that changed the world".

Britain

After the fierce French battle, Ascari achieved pole position at Silverstone with the intention to avoid the performance rise of Maserati and Ferrari, who achieved the second and fourth positions in the class alongside Jose Froilan Gonzalez and Fangio. Hawthorn is, in contrast, ranked third.

In the race itself, the battle was between Ascari and Fangio and ended with a victory going to the Ferrari driver, who again triumphed over the Maserati race.

[26]

3rd was Nino Farina, and the fourth place went to Jose Froilan Gonzalez, the Ferraris are amidst the Maserati and Hawthorn after his victory in France He finished fifth.

Germany

In the race that ended the year, Ascari was leading by a 17.5-point advantage against second-placed Mike Hawthorn. It meant that he would become a winner within "green hell" and that Maserati was, following its tardy reaction, needed to win races in order to avoid a repeat Ferrari victory.

Ascari took pole position in the hope of declaring himself the champion. He was joined by Fangio being in the second place in the starting order.

Ascari was unable to secure another win following a mechanical issue in his car, as well as after an engine malfunction after he had taken Luigi's Ferrari.

It was a different Ferrari which finally took the win, this time that of Nino Farina, who was one second more than Fangio.

[27]

Mike Hawthorn finished third. That meant that, even though neither Fangio or the British driver had won, Ascari was mathematically proclaimed champion with just two races remaining after his excellent beginning in the race. The Italian driver also won his second world title in succession.

[28]

Swiss

The final race took place on the Swiss circuit in Bremgarten in Switzerland, in which Fangio was the winner over Ascari.

However, as in the previous season and the previous season, the Italian driver didn't lose any motivation or competitiveness despite his title and won the race by taking advantage of breaks in Fangio who was able to finish fourth, despite making use of his co-driver Felice Bonetto's car in an era where Maserati's reliability was not as high. Maserati was not enough to allow him to compete for the title.

Alongside Ascari's win, Ferrari dominated in Switzerland by winning a triple including Nino Farina, and Mike Hawthorn taking the podium.

Italy

The championship was over with his ninth race in Monza the race that was to end the championship with a stunning display. Ascari was able to secure a pole in his race against Fangio.

But, the race was extended to five riders who would form groups for the final lap. Between the two riders, Ascari and Farina were trying to win when Alberto Ascari

made an accident that ended his career by running out of the race. Farina had to adjust her approach to stay clear of Ascari which allowed Fangio to take over both of them and end with a win in a race that was already running late for Maserati.
[29]
The victory of Fangio helped him finish second on the standings final table, two points clear over Nino Farina. Mike Hawthorn finished fourth in his debut year at Ferrari with a better result than his teammate, Luigi Viloresi.

Final CLASSIFICATION 1953
(Drivers who earned points)
Alberto Ascari 34.5
Juan Manuel Fangio 28
Nino Farina 26
Mike Hawthorn 19
Luigi Villoresi 17
Jose Froilan Gonzalez 13.5
Bill Vukovich 9
Emmanuel de Graffenried 7
Felice Bonetto 6.5
Art Cross 6

Onofre Marimon 4
Maurice Trintignant 4
Sam Hanks 2
Duane Carter 2
Oscar Alfredo Galvez 2
Jack McGrath 2
Hermann Lang 2
Fred Agabashian 1.5
Paul Russo 1.5

1954
Argentina
It was 1954 when the world championship dropped Formula 2 regulations to use 2.5-liter supercharged engines. It wasn't the only major change made to the race. Alberto Ascari was unable to start the championship, and was later joined by various constructors. His position at Ferrari was taken by Argentine Jose Froilan Gonzalez.

The season began with Argentina and it was believed that even with having no Ascari The level of competition among Ferrari and Maserati was to remain and give way to an exciting fight throughout the entire year.

Nino Farina won the pole position ahead of his co-teammate Jose Froilan Gonzalez, which could mean that Ferrari started the race with more strength than Maserati.

But once was in the competition, Fangio's skill changed the course, and he took the win, which was the first time for an Argentine in his home country.

[30]

The third and fourth places in the Grand Prix were awarded to Ferraris that included Nino Farina Jose Froilan Gonzalez and Maurice Trintignant, which demonstrated the power that the group has, and Maserati further in the back (between sixth and eighth following Elic Bayol's Gordini and the Gordini of Elic Bayol). Only the skill of Fangio could bring victory to Maserati. Maserati on the track in Argentina.

Indianapolis 500

Like previous editions, the race that was a mythical one was not relevant in this year's Formula 1 championship, with the new race winning in the hands of Bill Vukovich.

Belgium

At Spa the trend from the beginning of the season was maintained in Spa, with Fangio winning pole position over his Ferraris Jose Froilan Gonzalez and Nino Farina.

In the beginning, Fangio lost positions and his fellow racer Jose Froilan took the first spot, but shortly thereafter, Fangio had to withdraw due to a malfunction in the Ferrari. Fangio took the lead once more, but a damaged visor strap forced him to the pits. But, it didn't take too long to get back to his starting position.

Nino Farina was also forced to quit due to a breakdown, making Hawthorn as the sole rival to Fangio. Fangio was the only other competitor. Briton lost speed and and it slowed down and was pulled from the vehicle in a stupor. The driver was substituted by Jose Froilan Gonzalez, in the car that suffered a breakdown, which caused smoke to fill the cabin, which caused Hawthorn to fall unconscious. Fangio was left with no his closest competitors and was able to score an easy win, the second win of the season.

[31]

The many retirements enabled riders who were not as well-known to the racer like Maurice Trintignant in second place and

Stirling Moss' first big victory in third place in the private Maserati to finish on the top spot on the podium.

Jose Froilan Gonzalez, with Hawthorn's car, and despite the issues, was fourth place.

France

It was in France, Mercedes returned to the market after World War II with the distinctive Mercedes-Benz W196 due to its aerodynamic design. It also has an 8-cylinder injection engine. The appointment to Juan Manuel Fangio was surprising after he had completed the two races he had won with Maserati and Maserati, he was on to join the new manufacturer.

With the expectation of knowing how this new changes would impact the championship and the championship, the Mercedes started to take off at the circuit of Reims-Gueux.

The race was not just about having Fangio claim pole and his co-pilot Karl Kling took second starting position, making a stunning debut for his German constructor. Alberto Ascari, who also led a dramatic comeback assumed the place that Fangio quit in

Maserati getting third in the overall classification.

The race was a success, Mercedes's pace was also faster in the race, with Fangio and Kling being the most notable among the other competitors. Hawthorn's car went up in flames, and Ascari did not finish at least one full lap. The final race of Fangio Kling and Fangio Kling was extremely close and the Argentine took the win with a tiny tenth an advantage on his rival. They were taking the field together and winning a double in Mercedes debut.

[32]

Britain

The day before at Silverstone, Mercedes had already fulfilled all of its potential goals and the challenge was whether it could continue to dominate throughout the race. On the other hand, Maserati participated with up to 9 vehicles, trying not to lose its place.

Fangio was able to take pole position over his fellow Ferraris that included Jose Froilan Gonzalez and Hawthorn as well as Stirling Moss qualifying fourth for Maserati.

Even though Fangio continued to set records for speed, by having the Maserati reaching the 100-mph mark at Silverstone however, the race was won by Jose Froilan Gonzalez who stood out in the long-run to take the win by clinching victory with Ferrari.

[33]

Although he was the fastest driver, Fangio collided with oil drums multiple times and ended up finishing 4th in the event. This enabled Ferrari to achieve the double by winning second in the race from Mike Hawthorn and to put Argentine Onofre Marimon on top of the podium alongside Maserati.

The championship was halfway over, Fangio comfortably led the overall standings, and he even surpassed Jose Froilan Gonzalez in points.

Germany

To race at this race at the Nurburgring track, Mercedes evolved its Mercedes W196 to an open-wheel version in order to make it more competitive with Ferrari who won the race last year.

Practice before the race, tragedy brought the race to a close by the Argentine Onofre Marimon leaving the track along with his Maserati and falling down an embankmentand crashing into the ground, flipping the car, causing the death of his driver, the first fatal crash of Formula Championship. Formula Championship. 1. In the wake of this accident, Maserati drivers Luigi Villoresi and Ken Wharton decided not to take part in the race.

[34]

Fangio and Kling started leading the race, and were followed by Jose Froilan Gonzalez, who was so saddened by the passing of Marimon that, on lap 16, he decided to loan his car to Hawthorn to go on, as there was an accident in his.

Fangio was able to secure the victory in Germany and his teammate Kling falling to fourth. Hawthorn along with Gonzalez's vehicle finished second. The top three were completed with Frenchman Maurice Trintignant, with Ferrari.

Following having completed the German tests, Fangio was even more than the leader in the championship, with 19 points in the lead.

Swiss

In Switzerland the final race in the calendar Fangio had the option of declaring himself champion to the extent that it was enough that he won the race, or for Gonzalez to not be triumphant from it.

Jose Froilan Gonzalez achieved the pole ahead of Fangio trying to stop his fellow countryman from claiming his championship ... however, during the final race Fangio presented a thrilling driving demonstration that led the race from beginning to finish and even doubling the second class, and claiming the world's second championship and a season where he competed in two teams: Officine Alfieri Maserati and Daimier Benz AG.

[35]

With no excitement on the front the fight the duo of Stirling Moss and Mike Hawthorn who fought a thrilling fight until Moss's engine broke down. Hawthorn was then faced with fuel issues, allowing Jose Froilan Gonzalez to finish in second place, which did not allow him to win Fangio's title in the world championship.

The German Hans Herrman finally managed to finish on the podium alongside Mercedes.

Italy

With the world title taken by Fangio and Mercedes The Argentine was not content and continued to fight for dominance. In this manner the Argentine won pole position and won a second time by doubling the grid.

[36]

Hawthorn was second, with Jose Froilan Gonzalez third (after having occupied Umberto Maglioli's car) On a podium topped by Ferrari.

Alberto Ascari had to retire during a turbulent year. His ambition was to join Lancia and Lancia, which prevented him from participating in the championship. As a result, Ascari had to retire in France and Great Britain with Maserati, and is now doing it with Ferrari. In reality, he'd take on Lancia in the final event ... and it would be impossible for him to finish it.

Following this year's Monza event, Jose Froilan Gonzalez occupied an impressive second position. only third place was left to be decided. It was an extremely fought race among Frenchman Maurice Trintignant and Mike Hawthorn.

Spain

The championship ended in the Pedralbes circuit, with the sole concern of who would be third at the conclusion of the season. In Spain came the final race of Lancia who had an engine that was 90 degrees and that took pole by Alberto Ascari.

But in the race, they both had reliability issues Alberto Ascari's Lancia had a problem with the clutch, while Luigi Villoresi's had brake issues and neither could finish the race.

Following that, the pilots who had achieved the top position had mechanical issues, like Stirling Moss or the Frenchman Maurice Trintignant who thus made it possible for Hawthorn to aim for third position in the final ranking.

The race turned into a battle with Fangio and Hawthorn however, Hawthorn won the

race, but the Argentine was suffering from oil loss issues that led to him falling to third. Mike Hawthorn managed to lead the race until the end and take his second victory of his career and third at the close of the season.
[37]

FINAL CLASSIFICATION 1954
(Drivers who scored)
Juan Manuel Fangio 42
Jose Froilan Gonzalez 25.1
Mike Hawthorn 24.6
Maurice Trintignant 17
Karl Kling 12
Bill Vukovich 8
Hans Herrmann 8
Luigi Musso 6
Nino Farina 6
Jimmy Bryan 6
Roberto Mieres 6
Jack McGrath 5
Stirling Moss 4.1
Onofre Marimon 4.1
Robert Manzon 4
Sergio Mantovani 4
Prince Bira 3

Umberto Maglioli 2
Andre Pilette 2
Luigi Villoresi 2
Elijah Bayol 2
Mike Nazaruk 2
Troy Ruttman 1.5
Duane Carter 1.5
Alberto Ascari 1.1
Jean Behra 0.1

1955
Argentina
The 1955 year was re-established in Argentina with no major changes including Juan Manuel Fangio being the competitor to beat in the Mercedes 196 championship, while Ferrari being the best team that kept its principal team members Nino Farina Jose Froilan Gonzalez and Maurice Trintignant in a template which could see as many as 10 drivers during the entire season.

The most famous transfer was Stirling Moss, who left an injured Maserati to join his Daimier Benz AG team with Fangio.

In a grand prix that was held in hot temperatures, Ferrari struck first with

Gonzalez's pole. Ascari then made a solid start to Lancia as well as Fangio third.

Juan Manuel Fangio was the sole rider who was solo who completed 96 laps on the Autodromo Municipal de la Ciudad de Buenos Aires and win victory and kicking off the season in a dazzling way.

[38]

Second place was won by the Ferrari that was shared with Gonzalez, Nino Farina and Trintignant. Third was another Ferrari which Farina and Trintignant also shared with Umberto Maglioli, as part of an exchange of drivers that was never ever seen in competition.

The fourth spot was split between three drivers In this instance, Mercedes shared the vehicle with Hans Herrmann, Karl Kling and Stirling Moss.

Roberto Meires was the only driver aside from Fangio who completed in the same car however, he did it with five laps shorter that the race winner.

Monaco

Following a race as tough as Argentina's, a race that was no more difficult race was the second race for the year: Monaco.

Fangio won the pole this time around and Mercedes took the lead in the opening part of the race, with Stirling Moss following the Argentine. A transmission issue forced Fangio to pull out in the middle of the race to Moss. After the test and with race almost over The engine on the British car burst, taking the win.

This led to Ascari in the lead alongside Lancia However, an oversight in the chicane that was at the end of the tunnel led to an accident that saw Alberto Ascari was thrown into the water and was forced to swim away. It was the final race for Ascari, the Italian driver on the track in Formula 1, since a week later, he passed away while in testing an Ferrari sports car in Monza which ended his racing career through misfortune, and thus putting an end to the career that of one of the renowned racers in the world championship. .

Maurice Trintignant was then the new leader. And the Frenchman was able to win the race winning his first time on the track in Formula 1, accompanied on the podium by Eugenio Castelloti's Lancia and the

Maserati shared by Jean Behra and Cesare Perdisa.

[39]

Indianapolis 500

As with other occasions it was this was one of the times that the 500 Miles were not decisive for the Formula 1 championship although it was still a scoring race, because teams didn't want to take on the costs of the transfer was.

This race will be famous for the tragic accident that killed Bill Vukovich, when he had the chance to attain the record of winning three times consecutively in the infamous race.

Belgium

In Spa-Francorchamps Lancia ended up with Eugenio Castelloti as their sole driver. He took the pole position for a team that there was a lot more expected than he actually achieved in the race.

Castelloti broken the gearbox during lap 16, which ended Lancia's chances of winning as well as making the race more enjoyable for Mercdes who achieved an easy double, with winning race of Fangio as well as second at the second place finish for Stirling Moss.

[40]

In the background of Mercedes were behind them were the Ferraris from Nino Farina as well as the Belgian Paul Frere, in an year when the Italian team appeared to not meet the standards of previous seasons.

Holland

It was the Dutch Grand Prix was the following race following Le Mans. Le Mans disaster that forced an overhaul in the schedule. In the famous Le Mans test, driver Pierre Levegh collided with Lance Macklin who was torn from the stands in a crash which resulted in the deaths of both Levegh and the 83 people who were watching in one of the most tragic automobile accidents ever recorded.

Following this incident the circuits were re-evaluated and excluded from the championship circuits that were not considered to be safe This meant that an initially scheduled schedule with 11 events was cut down to seven tests and that a number of race tracks were not employed.

In the sporty part Zandvoort's professional career came to an end with a new dominance of Mercedes and a brand new win for Fangio after a fierce battle with co-pilot Stirling Moss whom he only exceeded by three tenths thanking him for the thrilling fight in the race.

[41]

With only two races left following the calendar shift, Fangio was comfortably leading the race with 27 points in front of Moss with only 13 points.

Britain

In the penultimate race on the Aintree circuit in Liverpool, Fangio had the first chance of being declared the world champion once more. Yet again, Mercedes once again dominated the race, with no rival to this German manufacturer.

But the dominant and pole position of this race was awarded to Stirling Moss, who thus gained his first win on his land, before Fangio.

It was believed that the Argentine allowed his opponent to win in order to be able to celebrate with his teammates which Fangio has categorically denied.

[42]

In spite of Moss's win the second place finish of Fangio's gave him enough points to again become a world champion. He took home the third title of his career. It was his second title in consecutive years.

This was the case for Mercedes throughout Great Britain was absolute, as Karl Kling accompanied Fangio and Moss on the podium and fourth was an achievement for that Mercedes that was driven by Italian Piero Taruffi.

Italy

At the time of the race at Monza, Fangio was already champion, and Stirling Moss had secured the third place. The primary focus was the battle for third place among Maurice Trintignant and Nino Farina who was just one point in front.

Mercedes continued to enjoy a spectacular year. Even though Moss was forced to pull out because of a mechanical issue however, this did not stop Fangio from winning a second win with Aerodynamic versions of Mercedes and was later followed by Piero Taruffi.

[43]

Jean Behra and the Argentine Carlos Menditeguy achieved fourth and fifth positions for Mercedes but just the Italian

Eugenio Castelloti was able to be third among German cars on the new podium in an annual season for Ferrari. Ferrari team, taking an impressive third position in the championship place above Trintignant as well as Farina.

Final CLASSIFICATION 1955
(Drivers who scored)
Juan Manuel Fangio 40
Stirling Moss 2. 3
Eugenio Castelloti 12
Maurice Trintignant 11.3
Nino Farina 10.3
Piero Taruffi 9
Bob Sweikert 8
Roberto Mieres 7
Jean Behra 6
Luigi Musso 6
Karl Kling 5
Jimmy Davies 4
Tony Bettenhausen 3
Paul Russo 3
Paul Frere 3
Johnny Thomson 3
Jose Froilan Gonzalez 2
Cesare Perdisa 2

Luigi Villoresi 2
Carlos Menditeguy 2
Umberto Maglioli 1.3
Hans Herrmann 1
Walt Faulkner 1
Bill Homeier 1
Bill Vukovich 1

1956
Argentina

Argentina was yet again the prize of the year that began a season whose biggest surprise was Mercedes dropping out of the world championship following two consecutive wins to claim the title, just as Alfa Romeo had already done prior to the start of the season.

The triple champion Fangio without any team, and Ferrari was not hesitant to make an offer which the Argentine took up. The Italian team also purchased the Lancia cars that were not able to win the championship. This is how Ferrari became the preferred constructor for the upcoming season.

In the qualifying phase, Jean Behra surprised by winning pole position, but his race was followed by the three Ferraris of Luigi Musso, Castelloti and Fangio.

Ferrari eventually won in the final race. However, they it had to do it using the car shared between Italian Luigi Musso and the current champion Fangio.

[44]

After the failure of Fangio's gas pump, which forced him to stay with Musso's vehicle and failing Castellotis' gearbox along and Peter Collins' accident, Ferrari did not show its dominance as the top spot was topped by two Maserati and one from Jean Behra and that of Mike Hawthorn, in a race where only the two manufacturers competed.

Monaco

At Monaco, Ferrari did get the pole position through Castelloti. Stirling Moss, who was racing with Maserati this year, finished 2nd on the grid.

The race ended when Eugenio Castelloti's Ferrari broke the clutch, which caused the Italian to be stranded in Fangio's carand for the Argentine to get past Peter Collins's vehicle.

These changes weren't enough to defeat an Stirling Moss that achieved victory by using its Maserati.

[45]

The car used with Fangio and Collins finished second, while the top spot was split by Frenchman Jean Behra with a Maserati that was capable of competing with Ferrari.

Indianapolis 500

1955 500 Miles were the first without the American Automobile Association (AAA) organisation following Le Mans' disaster and Vukovich's death. Le Mans disaster and Vukovich's death.

Despite the torrential rainfall, the race track was washed up in record time and, in addition to the fact that it was restored the year before in the end, it was finally in the conditions to host an event that was to remain unnoticed by Formula 1 teams, with the victory of Pat Flaherty.

Belgium

In Spa-Francorchamps Fangio was the first to take pole position with more than five seconds advantage during the rain, however his poor start saw him fall to fifth in the early stages of the race. In just five laps the

Argentine had already recovered the lead of the race.

Moss was Fangio's primary rival until he was unable to replace the rear wheel, following which Collins was able to move into second position. A fault within the gearbox of Fangio enabled him to surpass Collins, eventually securing his British victory.
[46]
The second place went to the Ferrari of Belgian Paul Frere, while Stirling Moss, despite his difficulties, made it to the top of the podium following his win in Cesare Perdisa's Maserati.

France

In the race at Reims-Gueux, Ferrari showed its authority by claiming the top three positions on the grid, including Fangio, Castelloti and Collins. In actual fact, Maserati appeared to lose performance, and its spot was given to the Vanwalls consisting comprising of Harry Schell, Colin Chapman and Mike Hawthorn starting fourth, fifth and sixth.

The Vanwalls had a disastrous race and had a bad race, with Chapman getting injured,

Moss breaking the gearbox and Schell breaking the engine.
This enabled Ferrari to achieve the comfortable double. an impressive win for Peter Collins, followed by Eugenio Castelloti. [47]
Fangio was fourth and was overtaken by Jean Behra's Maserati. Moss after shattering the gearbox and bringing Perdisa's car, was fifth.
There are only three races left remaining, Peter Collins took the first spot in the general classification, with 19 points. Jean Behra was second, with just one point advantage over Fangio and this is in turn, with only one point advantage. About Moss.

Britain

At Silverstone It took Stirling Moss who took pole with a nearly identical time as Fangio. Mike Hawthorn came out third following his switch to BRM.
The race was a disaster. Moss also ran into mechanical problemswith the rear axle of his Maserati that forced Moss to pull out with seven laps remaining. This enabled Fangio to finish the race with ease by doubling his competitors.

[48]
The second came Peter Collins, who after encountering issues with his oil pressure, he took his car from Alfonso de Portago to maintain the top spot in the overall classification. He is now just one point behind Fangio.

The podium was complete through Jean Behra with Maserati, in a season that was productive for the Frenchman.

Germany

Absolute equality between Fangio and Collins and Collins, the penultimate event of the year at Nurburgring. The rivalry between the two was evident during qualifying, with Argentine finishing on pole with just three tenths advantage over Collins. British.

The problem was that Collins did not manage to complete the course. First because of the loss of fuel in his vehicle following an accident in which he was involved in taking the vehicle of Alfonso dePortago. In the absence of Collins, Fangio achieved one more win in relative peace and was advancing towards an all-time world record.

[49]

Italy

Monza was the track that would determine the 1956 champion season. Prior to this race Fangio held the lead with an advantage of eight points against Peter Collins. The only way that could have allowed the Briton to be declared champion was to be the winner and to get the fastest lap as well as for Fangio not to finish the race.

On the other hand, Jean Behra was also only 8 points better than Fangio because of his incredible consistency, however with just the top 5 results registered in the race, the Frenchman was not a chance of winning the title.

Fangio's car exploded and broke the steering, and his demise would be one of prerequisites for Collins to become the world champion. Luigi Musso refused to give his Ferrari to Fangio to allow him to keep his title ... following which Collins himself in a show of true sportsmanship, loaned himself to offer his car to Argentine which cost him his world title. Fangio was, in

Collins his car, finished third, with three points with Collins, earning the Argentine the fourth title in the world championship and third consecutively.
[50]
Stirling Moss won the final race of the season, declaring himself the runner-up The race was won by Stirling Moss, and Collins placing third because of his gesture of respect to Fangio.

Final CLASSIFICATION 1956
(Drivers who scored)
Juan Manuel Fangio 30
Stirling Moss 27
Peter Collins 25
Jean Behra 22
Pat Flaherty 8
Eugenio Castelloti 7.5
Sam Hanks 6
Paul Frere 6
Paco Godia 6
Jack Fairman 5
Luigi Musso 4
Mike Hawthorn 4
Ron Flockhart 4

Don Freeland 4
Alfonso de Portago 3
Cesare Perdisa 3
Harry Schell 3
Johnnie Parsons 3
Louis Rosier 2
Luigi Villoresi 2
Hermano da Silva Ramos 2
Horace Gould 2
Olivier Gendebien 2
Dick Rathmann 2
Gerino Gerini 1.5
Landi Boy 1.5
Paul Russo 1

1957
Argentina
Argentina was again the first race of an upcoming season. the major news item was the removal from Fangio who was with Ferrari for a race with Maserati and taking over the role in the place of Stirling Moss, who passed to Vanwall who finally achieved his promise of giving him an automobile that could compete throughout the year.

Ferrari thus, was only left to Peter Collins, Eugenio Castelloti and Mike Hawthorn as its main actors.

In the Autodromo de Buenos Aires, Moss won the the pole ahead of Fangio after a brief alert from Vanwall. However, during the race Stirling Moss damaged the accelerator pedal, causing him to stop during the first lap. This led to Castelloti as well as Jean Behra's Maserati to battle at the front of the race.

But, Fangio would end up being the first player to be selected and scoring his first win of the season, just one minute ahead of co-player Behra.

[51]

Due to Ferrari's troubles in the form of Collins, Musso and Hawthorn having clutch problems and Castelloti experiencing timing issues, Maserati achieved a great results in the race's first. To the two first positions from Fangio and Behra and the fourth and third of Carlos Menditeguy as well as Harry Schell were added.

It was the final race for Italian Eugenio Castelloti, who was a driver in Formula 1, since unfortunately his death would occur just a few days after he had tested the Ferrari during the race in Modena. Another Ferrari driver passed away shortly afterwards the Spaniard Alfonso de Portago, while taking part in the famous Mille Miglia race in a tragic beginning of an era to Ferrari's Italian team.

Monaco

The second race in the Championship Fangio was the first to take pole position but was quickly beaten by Stirling Moss and later by Collins. Moss was involved in an accident during lap 4 in which Collins tried to avoid and hit the wall and putting both of them out of the race.

This led to a win for Fangio who clinched his second victory, starting the year in the best way and on the way to winning a world title. [52]

The second spot was an impressive win for Vanwall however it will not be by Moss or Tony Brooks. The podium was won through Masten Gregory, and the anecdote about Jack Brabham pushing his Cooper beyond the finish the line due to fuel issues.

Indianapolis 500

Another year the famous North American test was scoring for the Formula 1 championship, without any championship teams wanting to take part, and with a victory for the local racer Sam Hanks.

France

France is the 4th race of the season following the suspension of Belgium and the Netherlands due to issues with fuel supply. The race took place on the public roads in Rouen-Les-Essarts.

Fangio was once again the fastest qualifier but, in the first lap, the race, he was beaten by his teammate Behra and later Musso. After the fourth lap the Argentine was already in the lead after finishing in the top position, and securing another win, and an entire win thus far this season.

[53]

Ferrari appeared to awaken in France and was able to make a splash with Luigi Musso, Peter Collins and Mike Hawthorn occupying from second to fourth, with the belief for the Italian manufacturer would arrive at the right time to challenge for a title that was controlled by Fangio.

Britain

At the Aintree circuit in Liverpool, Stirling Moss achieved the pole position for Vanwall who wanted to impress at home. He was beaten by Behra however, before the beginning on the initial lap Moss returned to the top spot.

But, he had to pull out of the pits because of mechanical issues, allowing the Frenchman to rejoin the front. Moss was then in his vehicle with Brooks, who was in the same team, to resume his ninth place.

Forward, Fangio and Collins abandoned due to mechanical issues and the leader's clutch went off, and Hawthorn cutting himself while stepping onto the wreckage of the broken.

Lewis-Evans led the race with Vanwall however, he was soon lost to Moss. The British manufacturer was dreaming of an unbeaten race on his home track at the time, but Lewis-Evans was also forced to pull out because of a damaged throttle, however Stirling Moss did manage to make it to the finish line to award the first win on the track in Formula 1 to a British manufacturer.

[54]

Ferrari however, despite being unable to win the race however, had a great race and placed Musso, Hawthorn and Trintignant (sharing the same car as Collins) in third, second and fourth place.

Germany

In the Nurburgring, Fangio achieved pole position. However, despite some problems during the beginning in the race returned to the lead in the third lap distancing himself from the rest of the field gradually.

The only driver who was capable of being able to chase Fangio could be Peter Collins, although the Argentine was gradually shifting further away ... up until the 1 minute 18 second pit stop ended his race.

On the track the Argentine was running at an astronomical pace and set fast lap after lap, and breaking the track record as many as 10 times. He was able to catch Collins once more, catch Collins and then win a race that will be known for being one of the best performances of Fangio's racing and the background of Formula 1 that, in addition, helped him mathematically to earn his fifth World Championship, and the fourth time in the same row.

[55]

Ferrari was forced to choose another plane, with no success however, it did get a decent result, including Hawthorn, Collins and Musso taking over the second and fourth place and Stirling Moss fifth for a Vanwall which failed to sustain the Great Britain success.

Pescara

The final event of the year took place in the Pescara circuit during a season that could bring two major prizes on Italian land. It was an 25.6 km circuit that was on public roads, and the longest race ever used in the Formula 1 race.

Ferrari chose not to take part in this race in part due to the fact that Fangio was already a champion, and also as protest against the decision from the Italian government over its position regarding the banning in road race, specifically in the wake of the death of their driver Alfonso de Portago. The only exception was that Luigi Musso managed to participate in the test with the Ferrari as an individual driver.

Luigi Musso himself took first place in the race early on despite Fangio's pole, but was beaten by Moss in the 2nd lap.

The tenth lap was the one where Musso's engine caught fire because of the extreme temperatures, which caused Fangio to slide across the track with debris, causing damage to the wheel.

This provided Stirling Moss such an advantage that he won the race with ease.

[56]

Italy

Another time, Monza ended a championship where only the winner had to be determined. The final standings were favoring Moss by 17 points ahead of Luigi Musso's 16 points, with Mike Hawthorn also with options with 13 points.

Vanwall was extremely strong in qualifying, and occupied the top three spots on the starting grid alongside the British drivers Stuart Lewins-Evans Stirling Moss and Tony Brooks and was and then Fangio.

The Vanwalls split in the beginning and Behra and Fangio's Maserati from Behra and Fangio joined the Vanwalls to fight for the head to Moss as well as Behra.

Mechanical issues meant that the Vanwalls of Lewins Evans and Brooks were forced to end the battle, and Moss being chased by the Maseratis of Behra and Fangio while the French were forced to pit their cars shortly after.

Stirling Moss was able to keep Fangio from slipping behind, winning another victory over his greatest opponent. In the current season they shared all the wins of the championship.

[57]

Ferrari finished on top of the podium thanks to German Wolfgang von Trips, during a season that ended without a win in the favor of the Italian team. This proves that it was the right decision to Fangio to make the switch to Maserati.

In the final days of the season, Argentine Juan Manuel Fangio announced his retirement, or at the very most, throughout the entire season after winning five world championships. He also had the added pressure to have achieved these with four distinct manufacturers: Alfa Romeo, Mercedes, Ferrari and Maserati.

[58]

Maserati was, on the other hand, was pulling out due to economics. The year 1957 also was the final year in which it gave points to pilots who were in the same vehicle.

FINAL CLASSIFICATION 1957
(Drivers who scored)
Juan Manuel Fangio 40
Stirling Moss 25
Luigi Musso 16
Mike Hawthorn 13
Tony Brooks 11
Masten Gregory 10
Harry Schell 10
Sam Hanks 8
Peter Collins 8
Jim Rathmann 7
Jean Behra 6
Stuart Lewis-Evans 5
Maurice Trintignant 5
Wolfgang von Trips 4
Carlos Menditeguy 4
Jimmy Bryan 4
Paul Russo 3
Roy Salvadori 2
Andy Linden 2

Giorgio Scarlatti 1
Alfonso de Portago 1
Jose Froilan Gonzalez 1

1958
Argentina
In 1958, the most notable change was the introduction for the Constructors' World Champion, meaning that the prize could no longer be solely for drivers, but it would be a second race for the manufacturers to battle with each other. Additionally, the events were cut to an maximum of 300 kilometers in length, or 2 hours. It was the World Championship began once again in Argentina in the year 2000, and even though Fangio had declared his retirement in his entire season, he chose to compete in the World Championship with Maserati. Fangio began fourth on the grid, along with co-pilot Behra on the pole and also those with Ferraris were Collins as well as Hawthorn.

Fangio did not manage to increase his position in the standings during his race and finished in fourth place.

The victory was instead given instead to Stirling Moss in a Cooper in a Cooper Vanwall did not take part in the first race. In his first race, the winner was Fangio and, without him for the remainder of the season Moss wanted to be able to claim to the title which had been denied him at times amid an era of Argentine star.

[59]

After the failure on the back axle Collins' Ferrari, the Italian team was able to hold the last two spots on the podium thanks to Luigi Musso and Mike Hawthorn and began the season the way it finished the previous year, which was with the same positions as before and below, but without a victory that they were unable to achieve.

Monaco

In the wake of returning Vanwall back to competition, Tony Brooks achieved pole position for the Principality race, but he was beaten by Jean Behra's BRM prior to the beginning. He remained in the lead until a brake malfunction led to Hawthorn to overtake Brooks in the Ferrari 246.

Stirling Moss fought against Hawthorn however both retired due to mechanical

issues. The second of the remaining of the race was Maurice Trintignant who achieved the victory alongside Cooper and was the second time in succession to Rob Walker Racing. Rob Walker Racing team, which was the most impressive performance of a private-team during the entire history of Formula 1. The Cooper-Climax impressed with the rear-engine, which was a major surprise. Their triumph marked the beginning of the ending of front-engines.
[60]
Ferrari returned to take the top spot with Luigi Musso and Peter Collins as usual, in their inclination to race at the top levels, but not able to show their potential in wins.

Holland

On Zandvoort. Zandvoort track, Vanwall once again dominated the standings, claiming the top three positions on the grid, along with Lewis Evans, Moss as well as Tony Brooks.

Brooks and Lewis-Evans both had to quit due to engine issues however, the gifted Stirling Moss managed to lead Vandervell Products' Vanwall VW5 to victory.
[61]

It was this time not Ferrari that topped the podium, with Hawthorn fifth place as the fifth best placed but it was BRM Drivers Harry Schell and Jean Behra in third and second place respectively.

While this was happening, Maserati continued to fall to pieces without seeing any noticeable improvements in the beginning to the year.

Indianapolis 500

In this particular race, the most famous of all and with no full schedule to compete in this year's Formula 1 championship, Fangio wanted to be a part of the race however, after conducting tests with Kurtis Kraft's 500G Offenhauser team, which had a car that had a carburetor and chassis problem as high as 6 km/h lower than the top vehicles and did not show up to qualify.

The ultimate victory went to Jimmy Bryan.

Belgium

The harshness of Spa-Francorchamps race was felt this year when the two first drivers who crossed the finish line damaged vehicles. The first is Tony Brooks, who had been on the final lap due to gearbox issues. The Briton was able to win his first win on his own and the first one was achieved through the donation of his car for Stirling Moss.

Second place went to Mike Hawthorn with a Ferrari that was struggling to get to the top and third place went to Lewis Evans in a superb beginning to the season for Vanwall.
Belgium was also the first to witness the participation of a woman to Formula 1, Maria Teresa de Filippis who raced in the private Maserati 250F and finishing the race in tenth.

[63]

France

At the circuit of Reims-Gueux, Fangio returned in one of his appearances at the championship, but not having the same success as previous years , he was driving an Maserati that wasn't getting much attention.

In actual fact, Mike Hawthorn, who was leading the race was able to slow down the pace to ensure that Fangio didn't end up being doubled, and the Argentine was able to finish the race on the same track as the leader, thereby acknowledging his gratitude to his five times champion. Hawthorn finally took home the race that was long-awaited by Ferrari and was able to return to the winning road.

[64]

Wolfgang von Trips was third to boost Ferrari's excellent result Then Stirling Moss managed to finish second in the Vanwall.

The race, however, was marred by the tragic accident that killed Luigi Musso. The Italian quit the track after being thrown from the vehicle. He suffered serious injuries which would result in his death the next day in the hospital. This would be the first of many tragedies which would mark the 1958 season.

[65]

Britain

In Silverstone, Stirling Moss took the pole, though the race was not his to make the most of it due to a damaged motor in the Vanwall. In the absence of any competition with Moss, Ferrari took over the race and scored the double, and Peter Collins taking the win and Mike Hawthorn in second.

[66]

Roy Salvadori got the podium for Roy Salvadori was a BRM which had specific success and an impressive performance throughout the entire season.

With just four rounds left to be completed on a race schedule that spanned to 11 races Mike Hawthorn led the championship with 30 points.

For the constructors, Ferrari's consistency helped him to be ahead by 11 points over Vanwall who was battling Cooper only with two points in the gap.

Germany

At the Nurburgring Formula 2 teams that were racing who were racing under Formula 2 regulations were allowed to race with the intention of increasing the number cars on the grid. While both categories competed simultaneously, Formula 2 did not get to compete in the championship.

Mike Hawthorn achieved pole for Mike Hawthorn's Ferrari which was beginning to make an impression, but after 11 laps, he was forced to stop due to a clutch problem.

The war for supremacy occurred among Tony Brooks and Peter Collins and ended in a tragic outcome. Peter Collins' Ferrari

crashed into a ditch, and he was torn up and hit a tree. He sustained fatal injuries in a hospital accident that was similar to the one of Musso's in France.
[67]
Brooks had a bitter win following which he told that he'd never seen anyone drive like the speed that Collins did it.

Roy Salvadori and Maurice Trintignant were the two runners-up in the standings for Cooper.

Portugal

With just three races left during the year, the gap in the standings between Hawthorn as well as Moss on the table was just 6 points. Ferrari's lead with Vanwall was cut to just 4 points, which tightened the championships in both.

The Boavista circuit in Porto was the main venue to fight in the World Cup, with Stirling Moss getting pole position and Hawthorn being in second place. The fight continued during the race, in which Moss was able to win a second time for Vanwall and a huge edge in comparison to Hawthorn's Ferrari.
[68]

Hawthorn was punished by the race officials for returning in a risky manner and in the wrong direction following a start, which resulted in him losing the seven points he scored in Portugal. But, Moss, who had observed the incident and didn't consider it to be dangerous and approached the judges and asked for his disqualification be reversed as an act of utter bravery that saw Mike Hawthorn regained his second position.

This enabled Hawthorn to remain 4 points clear of Moss which is a lead could have been lost had he received a the disqualification.

In terms of the constructors' championship, with two races left, Vanwall was ahead of Ferrari by only one point.

Italy

at Monza, Moss was on pole in an attempt to take victory from Hawthorn however, the gearbox on his Vanwall broke, making it hard to compete for the title during the final stretch of the year.

This provided Mike Hawthorn a great opportunity to claim the title, but he came in second place behind Tony Brooks. Moss's victory offered him the chance to win the final race in Morocco.

[69]

Tony Brooks' victory for Vanwall, even with Hawthorn's second-place finish in the race and Phil Hill's second place for Ferrari it did stop the Italian team's choices. Without the race that was last, Vanwall won the first constructors' title ever in Formula 1.

Morocco

The final racing of the season, in Morocco (unique at this particular location within Formula 1 history), Mike Hawthorn was 8 points ahead of Stirling Moss, being the favourite to take home the world driver title.

Stirling Moss again had a excellent race to win as well as the fastest lap, which earned him an extra point. However, Mike Hawthorn, aware of the chance to become the champion, finished second to be awarded the world title.

[70]

Phil Hill was also third with the Ferrari that, though not getting the constructors' title however, did achieve the satisfaction of having led Hawthorn to the title.

To his credit, Stirling Moss achieved his fourth consecutive title as a runner-up during an amazing career that had the title of world champion. He finished just one point ahead of Hawthorn If Had he not stepped up to help following his disqualification from Portugal the tournament, he might be the champion.

The unfortunate season came to an end with a mishap. In the engine room of Stuart Lewis Evans' Vanwall exploded causing serious injuries to the pilot. He passed away six days later during the most tragic year of the race.

[71]

FINAL CLASSIFICATION 1958
(Drivers who scored) (Drivers who managed to score)
(Builders)
Mike Hawthorn 42 Vanwall 48
Stirling Moss Ferrari 41 Ferrari 40
Tony Brooks 24 Cooper-Climax 31
Roy Salvadori 15 BRM 18
Peter Collins 14 Maserati 6
Harry Schell 14 Lotus-Climax 3
Maurice Trintignant 12 Porsche 0

Luigi Musso 12 Connaught-Alta 0
Stuart Lewis Evans 11 OSCA Stuart Lewis-Evans 11 OSCA
Phil Hill 9
Jean Behra 9
Wolfgang von Trips 9
Jimmy Bryan 8
Juan Manuel Fangio 7
George Amick 6
Johnny Boyd 4
Tony Bettenhausen 4
Jack Brabham 3
Cliff Alison 3
Joakim Bonnier 3
Jim Rathmann 2
Bruce McLaren 2

1959
Monaco
The most recent event of the decade took place in Argentina as the venue for the opening ceremony and started in Monaco. The event was not the only thing that stood out. The most important and tragic story was the absence of the present winner Mike Hawthorn, who three months after winning the title was killed in a car accident.

Additionally the constructors' champion Vanwall because of the high mortality rate from last season's competition, chose to pull out of the race.

On the other hand the complete retirement of Fangio who could not be able to compete in a full-time program or in certain races resulted in the fact it was clear that there wasn't racer on the grid.

In these conditions there was a chance for a season in which Ferrari did not have a rival to compete for the championship. drivers like Jean Behra, Phil Hill, Tony Brooks or Cliff Alison.

However they were British constructors, particularly Cooper with his innovative rear engine had performed admirably and were a good bet to be able to compete with the Italian team.

Stirling Moss achieved pole position in a highly competitive class among Cooper with Ferrari. However the Briton did not make it to the finish of the race due to transmission issues with just 19 laps remaining.

The race was between Brabham's Cooper and Tony Brooks's Ferrari. Brabham won the race by twenty seconds faster than Brooks and claimed his first win and the first for one of Australian racing in Formula 1.

[72]

Ferrari as well as Cooper was the sole two brands capable of winning the race. Frenchman Maurice Trintignant completed the podium with Cooper Fourth was Phil Hill with Ferrari and sixth and fifth included Bruce McLaren and Roy Salvadori (the latter was Cooper-Maserati).

Indianapolis 500

This year's edition of 500 Miles was once again uninterested in the principal Formula 1 teams who, for the third year running didn't even think about their participation. The race was won by Rodger Ward.

Holland

Qualification on the Zandvoort circuit revealed a shocking Pole for Swedish Jo Bonnier in a BRM P25 race, which resulted in a not less surprising win to Bonnier himself. He scored the first victory of his Owen Racing Organization team.

[73]

The podium was made with Brabham's Cooper and Masten Gregory The only two drivers to stay out of becoming doubled up by Bonnier. Moss was experiencing mechanical issues yet again, and was forced to stop because of a damaged gearbox.

Ferrari was the fifth and sixth positions for Behra as well as Phil Hill, as he observed the British brands surpass the Italian team.

France

In Reims. Reims track, Tony Brooks achieved pole position for the Ferrari team that didn't wish to give in to the pressures of British manufacturers.

The heat was extreme to the point that the car's parts became brittle and detached, forcing Masten Gregory to withdraw with cuts on his face as well as Graham Hill for having his radiator punctured.

Then, Tony Brooks led the race from beginning to end winning the French race and securing an important win for Ferrari despite getting the throttle stuck in the race's final laps.

France has produced a stunning performance for Ferrari and also took second place behind Phil Hill.

[74]

The third place finisher was Jack Brabham in the Cooper T51 who's consistency allowed him to win the race with a five-point lead in front of Tony Brooks.

In the meantime, bad luck remained in the wake of Stirling Moss who was disqualified to receive help in by pushing his BRM with gearbox issues.

Britain

The British test, which was being held within Liverpool in the Aintree circuit The Ferrari team was unable to participate because of strikes in Italy which prevented the proper change of team members to Great Britain.

Tony Brooks, in order not to forfeit his chances of winning the title of driver was granted a permit to drive alongside Vanwall however, he ultimately had to stop driving due to mechanical problems.

The battle for the victory was between British marques Cooper and BRM and, more specifically, among Jack Brabham and Stirling Moss. Brabham didn't offer any alternatives to win all laps, and he won the race that earned him an advantage by 13 points over the competition.

[75]

Brabham was able to win comfortably However, the battle for the second spot was intense among Stirling Moss as well as Bruce McLaren. Stirling Moss achieved second position during the last part of the race. However, Bruce McLaren would set the record as one of the youngest drivers to record the fastest lap with 21 years old and 322 days.

Germany

The race, which was that of the German Grand Prix was held in the AVUS in West Berlin, a public highway that consisted of a straight, long road that had a hairpin at one end and a sloping curvature that was banked at the other. This made it the most efficient Formula 1 race yet. For the first time in the history of the sport the race was comprised of two heats.

Ferrari came back to title after his absence from Great Britain and did so with great determination, achieving three times the power of its engine in an oval that is basically "two lengthy straights". Tony Brooks took the victory with his team-mates Dan Gurney and Phil Hill.

[76]

French former Ferrari driver Jean Behra had decided to race in Germany in the German championship with Porsche and Porsche, but he suffered an accident that killed him during the Formula 2 race leading up to the race, which led to the cancellation of Porsche entirely. This tragically ended the life of Jean Behra and the car race of a fantastic driver who was able to achieve nine podiums during the championship.

[77]

Portugal

With just three races remaining, Tony Brooks led the championship by four points ahead of Jack Brabham, both of who stood out from the others in the standings.

Cooper's part was equally impressive. Cooper also faced a difficult race with a five-point lead over Ferrari.

In Lisbon in the Monsanto circuit was the focus. Stirling Moss achieved pole position in the hope to join the race for the title in a class that saw at least four Cooper were able to get the top positions.

The Brit accomplished his goal and Moss won with a dominant win by doubling the other drivers adding 10 points to the second period of the season, which Moss was hoping wouldn't come too late to challenge for the title.

[78]

Jack Brabham had an accident that kept Brabham from taking part in the race and Tony Brooks finished ninth with five laps missing, allowing Moss to finish 9 1/2 points ahead of the lead.

Masten Gregory took second place at the end of the competition for Cooper Masten Gregory finished second for Cooper, while Ferrari was forced be content with third following North American Dan Gurney, remaining six points further behind Cooper in the standings.

Italy

At Monza With only two races remaining the tense battle for the title recommenced. Stirling Moss took pole, hoping to convert his victory into victory using an unstoppable strategy, believing that the lighter weight of Cooper allowed him to stay out without switching wheels.

Tony Brooks had to retire after the first lap because of a piston issue that was a significant defeat for their battle for the drivers ' championship as well as for Ferrari to win the constructors championship.

In the meantime, Moss's approach seemed to be on the right path, as he gained an advantage as the race advanced. Moss's wheels held up and he won the race by 46 seconds over Hill's Ferrari.

[79]

Moss won the race and gave Cooper-Climax required points to become constructors' champion , with only one race left, putting an end to Ferrari's hopes.

What was tighter the championship for drivers. Jack Brabham finished on the podium, and his 3rd place helped him stay in the lead but only 5 1/2 points better than Moss following winning the British victory. Tony Brooks had it a little more difficult however, for the first time since 1951, three drivers could be champions at the end of the racing of the season.

USA

The final race in the season of 1959 and of the decade, was performed within the United States at the Sebring circuit. It was held with the constructors ' title already acquired through Cooper-Climax however, the driver's title to be decided.

Brabham was able to get Brabham to finish third or second with the fastest lap as long as Moss didn't finish ahead of Brabham. The Brit had to win or to be second with Brabham ahead of him. To be his own man, Tony Brooks had to win and record the fastest time, with Brabham in third place or better and Moss not finishing second in the race with his fastest lap.

After a controversial qualifying , which saw Harry Schell achieving an inexplicable third position by using an obscure shortcut that could not be identified in the course until later, Moss was first to pole, then Brabham and Brooks fourth.

Stirling Moss began leading the race and quickly gained an advantage over Brabham and Brabham, which earned him the prized title of world champion. However, a malfunctioning gearbox ended his hopes and forced him to quit.

Tony Brooks, the other candidate for the title was smashed to the ground by his teammate Wolfgang von Trips, having to stop for two minutes in a pit stop, which threw off the race.

The scenario then changed into a smooth race for Brabham to win the title... but it was complicated when , with two laps left Brabham's Cooper was running empty of gas. Brabham reduced his speed as his Teammate Bruce McLaren to pass him. Maurice Trintignant also beat him as did Tony Brooks soon after.

Fortunately Brabham was not the only drivers were a bit behind however, Brabham's 4th place was enough to give Brooks the chance to become champion should he win the race. Brabham's car came crashing to the stop and he had to drive it without assistance in order to comply with regulations, and then uphill.

Tony Brooks failed to catch up with Trintignant Cooper as well as Bruce Mclaren. The former setting the record by becoming the youngest driver to win the race at the age of 22 and only 104 days.

Thus, Brabham entered the finish line in the direction of his Cooper to claim himself a world champion at the finale of the season and the decade.

www.ingramcontent.com/pod-product-compliance
Lightning Source LLC
Chambersburg PA
CBHW050403120526
44590CB00015B/1801